Police Leadership in a Democracy

Conversations with America's Police Chiefs

Modern Police Administration

PUBLISHED TITLES:

Police Leadership in a Democracy: Conversations with America's Police Chiefs
Jim Isenberg

Police Leadership in a Democracy

Conversations with America's Police Chiefs

Jim Isenberg, Ph.D.

CRC Press
Taylor & Francis Group
Boca Raton   London   New York

CRC Press is an imprint of the
Taylor & Francis Group, an **informa** business

HV
8141
.I75
2010

CRC Press
Taylor & Francis Group
6000 Broken Sound Parkway NW, Suite 300
Boca Raton, FL 33487-2742

© 2010 by Taylor and Francis Group, LLC
CRC Press is an imprint of Taylor & Francis Group, an Informa business

No claim to original U.S. Government works

Printed in the United States of America on acid-free paper
10 9 8 7 6 5 4 3 2 1

International Standard Book Number: 978-1-4398-0834-4 (Hardback)

Library of Congress Cataloging-in-Publication Data

Isenberg, James.
    Police leadership in a democracy : conversations with America's police chiefs / James Isenberg.
        p. cm. -- (Modern police administration)
    Includes bibliographical references and index.
    ISBN 978-1-4398-0834-4
    1. Police chiefs--United States. 2. Police administration--United States. 3. Police--United States. I. Title. II. Series.

HV8141.I75 2009
363.2068'4--dc22   2009010250

Visit the Taylor & Francis Web site at
http://www.taylorandfrancis.com

and the CRC Press Web site at
http://www.crcpress.com

Table of Contents

Modern Police Administration

The books in this series are each focused on a specific police administration topic. The premise of the Modern Police Administration series is simple: Today's police administrators, and those preparing for such responsibilities, although they are currently served by a handful of introductory texts, have access to few books that go into detail on specific topics such as police recruitment, managing training, police media relations, or managing Compstat. There may be a few articles on these topics, a training program or two, and some expert consultants, but little in the way of full-length documentation.

Back in the 1950s, 1960s, and 1970s, much of the early literature on policing was focused on police administration, including textbooks by the legendary O. W. Wilson and articles in such respected periodicals as the *Journal of Criminal Law, Criminology & Police Science*, and the *Journal of Police Science and Administration*. Pioneering college programs at Washington State University, Michigan State University, and a few other schools also focused on police science and police administration. During this professional era of police development, much of the emphasis was on figuring out how to run a police agency more efficiently.

But then the field shifted its attention. The focus of reformers turned to such key issues as racial discrimination, community relations, police discretion, and police use of force. Researchers began to study both individual police behavior and police strategies more closely. In higher education, degree programs evolved toward the broader perspectives of criminal justice and criminology, whereas police administration became nothing more than a single course, often an elective. Since the 1990s, the new strategies and paradigms of community policing, problem-oriented policing, and intelligence-led policing have dominated the attention of police executives, educators, and researchers.

These changes have been very good for policing and for communities. Police behavior today is better regulated than in the past, police use of force and pursuit driving are guided by careful policies and procedures, and police strategies are more often based on solid evidence about what works (and what doesn't). Police agencies are more diverse and more representative of their communities than ever before. The police field today is much more scientific, professional, and accountable than most other public services.

However, one other consequence of this policing evolution is that attention has been diverted away from the nuts and bolts of police administration—perhaps not so much in practice, but certainly in the policing literature and in higher education. Since the police field in the United States is such a big enterprise now, with 18,000 separate agencies and over 1 million employees, it would seem deserving of up-to-date books on important topics directly tied to managing police personnel and police organizations. Over the next few years, the Modern Police Administration series hopes to provide a range of such books.

Please encourage your police agency, police academy, police colleagues, university, and library to invest in this series. Our hope is that these books will become indispensable sources of the best thinking and best practices in police administration. Anyone who is serious about police administration should have ready access to this series.

Also, please let us know if you have suggestions for book topics and book authors. We know that there are many expert practitioners and expert trainers in the police administration field, and we hope to provide many of them with the opportunity to distill their knowledge and experience for the benefit of others.

The Modern Police Administration series is overseen by an editorial board representing many years of experience as police executives, professors, trainers, and consultants. Feel free to contact any of us with your ideas and suggestions.

Series Editor

Gary Cordner is professor of Criminal Justice at Kutztown University in Pennsylvania and a commissioner with the Commission on Accreditation for Law Enforcement Agencies (CALEA). Previously, he was police chief in St. Michaels, Maryland and dean of the College of Justice & Safety at Eastern Kentucky University, where he also served on the Kentucky Law Enforcement Council, the Kentucky Criminal Justice Council, and the Lexington/Fayette County Civil Service Commission. He is past president of the Academy of Criminal Justice Sciences and past-editor of Police Quarterly and the American Journal of Police. He earned his Ph.D. from Michigan State University.

GARY CORDNER, PHD
Professor, Kutztown University
Commissioner, Commission on Accreditation for Law
Enforcement Agencies (CALEA)

Deputy Editors

Theron Bowman, PhD
Chief of Police, Arlington, Texas
Commissioner, Commission on Accreditation for Law Enforcement Agencies (CALEA)

Ed Connors, JD
President, Institute for Law & Justice

Larry Hoover, PhD
Professor, Sam Houston State University
Past President, Academy of Criminal Justice Sciences

Gary Margolis, EdD
Research Associate Professor, University of Vermont
Commissioner, Commission on Accreditation for Law Enforcement Agencies

Darrel Stephens, MS
Director of State and Local Programs, Johns Hopkins University
Former Chief of Police, Charlotte–Mecklenburg, North Carolina

About the Author

Jim Isenberg is the director of strategic planning for the North American Family Institute. In this capacity, Dr. Isenberg directs the development and implementation of innovative, community-based programs serving adolescents in the juvenile justice, law enforcement and social services settings. He has extensive management, organizational development and program implementation experience in the fields of juvenile justice, youth services, corrections, law enforcement, social services and transportation.

In the criminal justice field, Dr. Isenberg has served as the special assistant for criminal justice to the Massachusetts Secretary of Human Services. He also served as director of planning for the San Francisco Sheriff's Department with a specific emphasis on the development of community corrections programs. Dr. Isenberg also has experience working with three urban school districts' school safety departments. He was project director for the national Police Corps program with specific focus on development of youth training programs, training of police trainers and leadership programs for police officers.

In addition to his criminal justice experience, he served as a senior executive with both the San Francisco and New York transportation systems. In this capacity, he directed the development of a human resources division and a marketing division. Finally, he has an extensive experience in the conflict resolution field in both domestic and international settings. Dr. Isenberg completed his PhD at the University of California in police leadership development.

Preface

This study describes the many leadership challenges confronting America's police chiefs. This book focuses on personal interviews with 26 American police chiefs. The group is composed of a diverse group of police leaders who discuss their leadership challenges in a wide array of cities (and may no longer be in the position they held when interviewed). The chiefs were interviewed about their leadership vision, successes, and challenges. The chiefs discuss their visions for their departments and the many issues they must address on a daily basis to achieve their goals.

In addition to my conversations with the chiefs, they also share their experiences about implementing these visions. The chiefs discuss their strategies for enforcing the law as well as collaborating with the communities in which they serve. The chiefs also discuss their ideas about police officer training, their challenges working with police unions, and their experiences working with mayors and other external political and community organizations. Finally, they examine the present dilemmas of police leadership and provide new insights about the future role of police leaders.

As the chiefs describe their experiences, they offer the reader an opportunity to learn about some of the specific challenges that police leaders in a democracy face. They talk of their efforts to build strong, positive relationships with their local communities while often facing resistance to this idea from within their own department. The chiefs also outline their strategies for enforcing the law and building a strong culture of accountability within their department. They outline their strategies for developing police officers while confronting recruitment issues and, in some cases, negative reactions to their visions from both their officers and the community.

Finally, throughout this study, I assess the chiefs' discussions carefully and offer a set of recommendations for the future of police leadership in a democracy. The recommendations incorporate the chiefs' perspectives and offer the reader an opportunity to implement new ideas for police leadership within the communities of America.

This book offers a unique opportunity to listen to police chiefs explain their problems, successes, and mistakes. The text focuses on key leadership challenges and offers the reader an opportunity to understand police leadership as well as formulate new approaches to developing police officers and police leaders in the future.

Acknowledgments

I appreciate the support of all members of my doctoral committee, with special thanks to William Ker Muir and Donald McQuade. Thanks to all of the police chiefs interviewed. I also thank Dr. Yitzhak Bakal; Dr. Gene Moore; Jay Paris; Jill Dichiara; my wife, Gail; and my brother, Steve.

Introduction

On a daily basis, the American media share their version of the role and behavior of police through news accounts or as part of a never-ending series of popular television dramas. The American public is bombarded with news stories about police officers' excessive use of force or the random violence they must confront on the streets of American cities. The police are presented one day as protectors of America's core values, whereas another day they are attacked for overstepping the bounds of a democratic state. Television leads most of its local evening newscasts with stories of shootings, robberies, and arrests of the "bad guys." After the news, prime-time crime shows highlight the thoughtful nature of police work, which is focused on carefully and persistently uncovering the special clues that lead to the identification and arrest of suspected criminals. Though the American public applauds the many constructive crime-reduction strategies of the police, the public has also witnessed the results of police corruption and failures of police leadership.

The American police saga does not stand alone; stories of police capabilities and inadequacies are omnipresent as headlines and commentators examine the counterterrorism efforts of the British police or the building of a police force in Iraq and other emerging democracies. The dilemmas of policing regularly carried by the news media or television dramas give the public a confusing perception of the role of the police. The stories told by police chiefs themselves in this book provide a realistic window on the day-to-day realities of police leadership in America or any other democracy.

Although there are many celebrated cases of police chiefs leading their departments in solving high-profile murders or dramatically reducing crime in their jurisdictions, the daily reality of their jobs involves constant pressures and challenges. Some chiefs have been confronted with their own deviant officers, who have either deliberately or unconsciously performed their duties in a way that has angered the community. People in communities formally or informally demonstrate their displeasure with overly aggressive arrest policies that target drinking in public, loitering, or dumping trash on the street. In the past decade, police chiefs have encouraged "community partnerships" with the police department, even though many in the community express distrust, if not disdain, for police behavior.

Police leaders and officers wrestle with such issues as judicial and community oversight, inappropriate use of force, the philosophical shifts of professional policing, and the daily rigors of providing police services in local communities. The rule of law, judicial oversight, and the norms of the community establish a framework for governing the local police institution in a democracy, but it is ultimately the chief who determines how these mandates will be developed and implemented within the police organization and the community.

The field of law enforcement has been evolving from a reactive to a preventive approach to reduce crime and improve community safety. This means continuing to address ongoing issues of crime while mobilizing support from the community for law enforcement and crime-prevention efforts. This is now taking place within the context of a post-9/11 world with the advent of sophisticated, modern technology.

Police leaders must maintain a balance between providing safety and law enforcement, and ensuring the protection of people's civil rights and liberties. This study will explore the specific organizational leadership and community issues that must be addressed by the chief to ensure that the community is safe and that its residents are afforded respect and decent treatment by its police officers. This important balance enables the police chief to maintain a leadership role in a community.

The critical role and behavior of police officers in American society has been thoroughly documented for over 50 years. What is not always well understood is that the person who leads the police department must make constant choices among a number of reasonable alternatives. These choices reflect changes in external contexts and events, evolving social philosophies and policies, and external and internal political pressures. The police chief is responsible for the overall direction of every police department in America.

A police leader is responsible for establishing a vision and mission for the department, creating strategies to implement that vision, building a team that supports the vision, and managing external and internal challenges and accountability for the successful implementation of the vision. He or she must recognize the strong values of the community and the importance of empowering police officers to meet the goals of the vision and mission of the department. The value of the departmental staff and the importance of input from the community must also be acknowledged and incorporated into the chief's vision. Perhaps the most important task of a police chief is to serve as the principal communicator, who must articulate the vision to both the department and the community. He or she must have the ability to not only teach, but also to actively persuade and mobilize support for the vision.

This book tells the stories of 26 American police chiefs, who come from diverse ethnic and racial backgrounds and a variety of departments and communities across the United States. The chiefs were selected to participate in these conversations because of their recognized experience as police leaders. Many of the chiefs have served in more than one city and others have been acknowledged as leading innovators in the field of policing. They bring their own personal experience and professional leadership style to the position. Many came to policing through their own choice, with no prior family involvement in the profession. Most have a college education and certainly place a very high value on both education and broad experience. Many worked and lived through events of the past 40 years and a few started their police careers following the serious civil disturbances in American cities in the 1960s and 1970s.

These 26 men and women offer insights into their experiences working in a range of communities, from major urban cities to smaller towns across the country. All recognize the serious challenges the United States faces around economic inequality and racial divisiveness, as well as the post-9/11 realities of terrorism and homeland security. Though all the chiefs generously offered an analysis of their departmental challenges, they also displayed gracious acceptance and reflection about the mistakes that had been made during their tenures. In most cases, the mistakes involved hiring the wrong person for the wrong reasons. Some admitted that their inability to build consensus for their vision or address serious challenges in a more thoughtful, timely manner led to their downfall. Whatever the case, all of the chiefs demonstrate an important quality that Martin Linsky and Ron Heifetz so ably underscore in their book *Leadership on the Line* when they trumpet the importance of "leadership adaptability."[1] The central values that distinguish this group of police leaders include adaptability, tenacity, and willingness to explore new frontiers.

Though their police jurisdictions were different, the chiefs universally agreed that the key elements of successful police leadership included creating a vision of policing in a democracy and developing strategies for implementing that vision. In addition, the chiefs clearly recognized the fundamental need to develop and support their police officers as well as building strong relationships with both the community and the political structure of the city.

Choices of Police Leaders in America

1

Policing: An Evolving American Institution

The vision of what a police department should be has evolved significantly over the past 100 years. In the early 1920s, police chiefs such as August Vollmer of Berkeley, California, were primarily concerned with the structure of their organizations. Vollmer is considered one of America's first professional police leaders. His focus on building a well-constructed, professional organization set the tone for police leadership all over the country. His vision was designed to combat corruption and community disorganization. The increased incidence of crime during what is known as the Progressive Era in the United States created a new mandate to deal with institutional development and serious corruption issues in police organizations. The Progressive Era was a pivotal period in American history during the early 1900s when new American public institutions, such as the police, were in the midst of reform and reorganization.

Vollmer introduced professional standards for recruit selection and officer training, recognizing that these two elements were fundamental to insuring the establishment of a professional police department.[1] He set up a training program that focused on the roles and functions of the officers, and ensured that there were clear policies regarding how the police should interact with the public. Prior to Vollmer's initiatives, most police departments operated within a patronage system and essentially allowed all situations to be handled according to the whims of individual officers on the beat. Though Sir Robert Peel in England had an initial vision of policing as early as the 1830s, it was Vollmer who set the standard for developing the profession in the United States.[2]

In 1931, President Hoover created the Wickersham Commission to confront an ongoing pattern of corruption and failure of police integrity. The commission was mandated to do a "searching investigation of the whole structure of our federal system of jurisprudence" with particular emphasis on police tactics in a democracy.[3] Though Vollmer had outlined some of the key tenets of police professionalism, the corruption and outrageous mismanagement of police departments in the late 1920s necessitated development of a set of professional standards that would guide the world of policing.

In the early 1950s, there was increasing recognition of the need for a strong centralized form of police leadership. Although the Wickersham Commission had made some progress to improve police management, there was still evidence of serious police leadership failures throughout the country. There was also concern that allowing uncontrolled police discretion could undermine the individual rights of citizens. Though the police leaders had tried to address the issues of professionalism and corruption for many years, the institution still lacked a clear professional foundation to manage the essential relationship between officers' discretionary power and the rule of law that was supposed to guide their decision making. Considerable attention was focused on judicial oversight of police officers in order to reduce corruption as well as overzealous behavior, while police chiefs were limited to managerial and technocratic duties. The chiefs' primary mandate was to prevent charges of police misbehavior while instituting policies and controls to prevent the inappropriate use of police discretion in the community. They had little interest in directly involving the community in any form of oversight or collaboration with their departments. The Los Angeles Police Department had set the standard for a legalistic model of policing, which emphasized professionalism and maintained only a minimal technical relationship with members of the community.

In the 1960s and 1970s, while police chiefs continued to focus on the need for improved efficiency and professional managerial excellence, many of the nation's police chiefs began to face direct challenges to their authority. In particular the public was reacting to the police response to civil rights, political, and Vietnam War demonstrations. Cities were erupting in riots that reflected the failure of American leaders to address the legitimate civil rights protections for all citizens. In cities such as Newark, New Jersey, and New York, challenges to police authority not only took place in the halls of the government but in the streets. The bloody confrontations between police officers and citizens underscored the breakdown of law and social order. In 1967, the President's Law Enforcement Commission stated that "the struggle to maintain a proper balance between effective law enforcement and fairness to individuals pervades the entire criminal justice system. It is particularly crucial and apparent in police work because every police action can impinge directly and perhaps hurtfully, on a citizen's freedom of action."[4]

There was considerable external pressure for greater community control of the police departments. Whereas some police departments considered establishing boards of citizens to provide institutional oversight, other departments completely rejected this concept. New internal strategies were initiated, including community relations units, designed to both mollify and engage citizens in a more positive relationship with their local police. Police leaders who had previously made every effort to maintain their distance from any community accountability were now faced with a new reality.

Politicians and community leaders began to demand a direct relationship with their police departments and their police leaders. Police chiefs could no longer maintain a posture of professional distance from the community; instead, they had to explore new policies and structures that would enable their departments to gain both respect and support from their local communities. At the same time, the collective concerns of police officers were being expressed internally with the onset of the police labor union movement.

In the 1980s and 1990s, the evolving police culture expressed formally through the new police unions questioned leadership as well as many of the new strategies for working with the community. Though maintaining professional distance had some value in reducing police corruption, it clearly had alienated many community members. Police officers had to struggle with the accepted internal norms around use of force as well as a profusion of unwritten rules within the policing community. Police leaders in cities across the country began to realize that there was a need for more creative efforts to manage the relationship between police officers and their communities. Program approaches such as community policing and problem-solving policing began to emerge. Research projects such as the Police Foundation's Kansas City Police Study highlighted the need for greater community participation and prevention-oriented efforts to reduce the spread of crime. This study had carefully assessed the Kansas City Police Department's allocation of police resources. The results of the study underscored that there was no clear method or logic for allocation of resources to prevent crime, but found that the police primarily only respond to crime after it had been committed.[5] However, the internal police culture was not prepared for community-oriented policing approaches, and police leaders found themselves caught in the middle between the community and their own officers. This balancing act requires an understanding of the culture, norms, and practices of the department. Working with the police culture remains a primary concern of police leadership.

The Rodney King incident and ensuing riots in 1992 in Los Angeles sparked a new community dialogue about police leadership. The issue of use of coercive force by police officers was at the top of the agenda, along with the need to improve community relations and protect individual rights. No longer could a police leader focus on managerial priorities alone. In Los Angeles as well as other cities, there had to be a clear organizational vision that included both the department and the community. As the realization of this vision emerged over the past 50 years, it was also clear that the formation of such a partnership was not always achievable. The history of police leadership in America was not a cumulative succession of distinct visions, but a continuing challenge that required police leaders describing a vision continuously during their tenures.

Leadership as a Balancing Act: "Walking the Razor's Edge"

In the present world of American policing, police chiefs face countless dilemmas as they try to clarify their mission regarding their departments' direction in the community. One of the biggest challenges is balancing political demands for law enforcement with the need to mobilize community support and maintain trust. In recent years, new challenges, such as terrorism and immigration, are further redefining police departments' missions. The very tenets of the role of police officers in a democracy have been central to discussing immigration, terrorism prevention, and crime reduction. The need to maintain the safety and security of the public while ensuring a respect for the rights of each individual creates dilemmas for police leaders on a daily basis.

Of course, police chiefs do not make such decisions in isolation and in fact have often had to negotiate with political leaders or superiors, such as the mayor and other constituencies, concerning values, constraints, and ground rules. Chiefs must juggle many external and internal political realities and policies, while maintaining support for their vision and ultimately the successful implementation of policing strategies in a local community. This study enabled police chiefs to tell their stories about the many dramas that unfold in meeting the internal and external challenges to their role and authority.

Central to the success of the police leader is developing a relationship with the community and establishing a vision that creates a clear mission to meet the needs of both the department and the community. Strong leaders are self-directed, but their understanding is formed by learning and their relationships with others. The impact of one's peers, mentors, and other personal influences ensures development of unique leadership styles. In these conversations with the chiefs, there was an opportunity for them to outline their personal influences and guidance in developing their leadership approaches. They described how they deal with specific crisis situations or built the capacity of their department to address new challenges, such as gang violence or changing community demographics. Chiefs spoke of their own leadership training and how they used the experience and writings of others in developing their style. The role of the police leader is demanding, sometimes frustrating, but at all times central to the life of the community.

Strategies to Reduce Crime While Protecting the Public

Once a police chief has articulated the vision and built consensus for the support of the mission, it is up to him or her to shape and manage strategies for the officers to implement it in the community. Studies, evaluations, and other performance indicators often drive strategies. For example, a fundamental finding of the Kansas City Police Study by the Police Foundation in the late 1970s was that "random motorized police car patrolling neither reduces crime nor improves the chances of catching suspects."[6] In fact, although "it used to be thought that saturating an area with patrol cars would prevent crime, it does seem to, but only temporarily, largely by displacing crime to other areas." Researchers also found that "police who ride in patrol cars, especially two-person cars, become rather self contained and remote."[7] Traditional patrol strategies were neither reducing crime nor reassuring potential crime victims, some of whom feared the police as much as they did the criminals.

Later in the 1990s, police leaders who had placed the majority of their efforts into organizing their departments to respond quickly to 911 calls began to recognize that a response approach was not having much impact on the crime rate. Their police officers were chasing calls and only dealing with issues after the crime had already been committed. Police leaders began to explore the possibility that police could actually prevent crime and ask how they might reorganize their departments to meet this goal. New strategies for crime prevention involved improved relationships with the community.

As a result of the critical feedback received during the 1980s and 1990s, new community-oriented, participatory, and problem-solving policing strategies evolved to manage the relationship between the police and their communities. These approaches emphasized mobilizing police officers to build partnerships with the community and gain support for prevention and problem-solving strategies. Police leaders also began to explore new methods of using data to identify crime patterns and improve accountability for crime reduction from department commanders. Police leaders have introduced the following four strategies across the country in the past 20 years: community policing, broken windows theory, problem-solving policing, and measuring performance and results internally. These strategies have become the core elements of police leaders' visions for providing safe American communities.

Community Policing

Community policing includes the concepts of police–community reciprocity, decentralization of command, reorientation of patrol, and generalized rather than specialized policing. These managerial approaches are directly linked with the police departments' overall efforts to communicate with the communities they serve. To facilitate this new level of communication, departments established specific geographic districts for patrol officers, created structures to ensure a regular flow of information between district officers and their communities, and developed an overall mission that underscored the value of positive police and community relations. The results of these efforts have been manifested in many cities by crime reduction, improved community support, and an overall redirection of the norms and values of the policing institution. Police leaders have embraced their positive relationship with the community because it provides institutional support and offers a clear direction for the allocation of police resources in the local community.

Broken Windows

In 1982 George Kelling and James Q. Wilson outlined their broken windows theory of crime prevention in *Atlantic Monthly* magazine.[8] This policing strategy sought to reduce crime by addressing the quality-of-life issues that irritate people in the community and indicate a breakdown of order in a neighborhood. It focuses on keeping the physical environment of the community safe and clean, and mobilizes the police force to identify issues such as public drinking in order to establish a strong set of norms that support a law-abiding, safe community. It also provided the framework for police accountability and strategic use of police resources. This approach has become one of the benchmarks for American policing in the new century.

Kelling introduced his theory to the New York City's transit system leadership, and it was applied in an urban environment that was besieged by graffiti, homelessness, and public safety issues. Kelling then joined with Police Chief William Bratton in implementing the broken windows theory in New York City. Their work led to a significant reduction of crime and an overall improvement of the perception of safety on the streets and in the subways of New York City. This theory was linked with zero-tolerance approaches to crime reduction and a new accountability structure that focused on the allocation of police resources to support crime prevention mandates from police leaders.

Problem-Solving Policing

In the late 1990s and into the new century, police leaders explored a problem-solving approach as a key component of the overall community policing strategy. Problem-solving models argue for more police discretion by the person on the beat rather than strictly through the rule of law.[9] The models highlight the role of the police officer as a participant within the community as well as a source of support even outside of the normal parameters of rule of law. In some locations, officers carefully track burglary patterns and create prevention plans to reduce the incidence of this crime. As one example of problem solving, the Charlotte–Mecklenburg (North Carolina) Police Department implemented a thoughtfully organized marketing campaign to remind people to close their garage doors, and the result of this problem-solving effort was a dramatic reduction of home burglaries. These types of participatory initiatives have become more engaging for police officers in the past 10 years as police leaders encourage problem-solving and community policing orientations to communities.

Expectations for police participation and, ultimately, resolution of community problems are not always clear or possible. Still, the police leader must be able to find and implement the appropriate approach to settle all matters effectively and respectfully.

Measuring Performance and Results Internally

The debate continues about the efficacy and value of community policing. The debate focuses primarily on the allocation of police resources and how to support both strict law enforcement and a problem-solving approach to crime prevention. The importance of a strong, positive relationship between the police and the community is a constant value. However, the bottom line is always how well the department is able to prevent crime and protect the public's safety.

The Compstat process of internal police accountability was introduced and championed by Chief Bratton in New York City and has become a central accountability tool for police executives.[10] The process brought police commanders together with other top police executives on a regular basis to examine in detail the specific crime patterns, incidents, and suspects that might be involved with criminal activities in police districts. Top police commanders carefully scrutinize strategies and tactics for crime intervention and prevention. In addition at these sessions, the commanders develop specific strategies for enforcement that are formulated at the Compstat sessions. Police leaders have used Compstat to measure their departmental performance as well as demonstrate the value of their prevention and intervention strategies to the entire community. Prior to the introduction of the Compstat model, police leaders monitored their officers' response to 911 calls and attempted to extrapolate information from reviewing the Part One crime data, which essentially tabulates only the more serious crimes that have been committed in a community. The Compstat model gave police leaders a tool that could both monitor local crime and nuisance incidents as well as help them prevent crime, rather than only react to it.

The Compstat approach had a significant impact on allocating resources for community policing. However, chiefs still face numerous external constraints, such as monitoring and oversight, conflicts with the courts and prosecutors, and debates about distribution of resources and application of the law. There have been mixed reactions within departments to the steady, focused review of police officer accountability through the Compstat process. Some chiefs believe the rigorous inquiries and emphasis on data and statistical outcomes can undermine officer morale. However, it remains the chief's responsibility to navigate the department on a steady course among a myriad of bureaucratic, political, and community needs and goals.

Communicating the Vision: Building and Managing a Team

Once a department vision and strategies have been identified, police leaders must be able to organize a team and build its capacity. They must enable the department to understand and value community goals and incorporate them within the department vision. The team also has to recognize the influence of the external political actors. Meeting the needs and expectations of the community in conjunction with the organizational and political goals of the department requires a delicate political and social balancing act. To meet the new challenges of terrorism prevention, emerging new immigration patterns, overall crime reduction, and mobilization of community support has required creating a new organizational capacity and style of police leadership.

Police leaders acknowledge the pivotal role that commanders and first-line supervisors perform in the organization. However, there has been limited success with the formulation of leadership and supervisory training approaches that adequately address the police supervision challenges. According to James Q. Wilson:

> Police patrol officers are members of coping organizations: their discretion is not easily limited by imposing rules. An excessive reliance on rules can lead to shirking or to subversion. To solve the problem of arbitrariness one must rely on effective management, especially on the part of first-line supervisors—sergeants and lieutenants.[11]

Few police leaders have been able to provide adequate leadership development to meet the supervisory challenges that face police officers on a daily basis. The challenge is to understand the variety of situations that police officers encounter and provide the executive leadership to ensure that a take-charge approach on the streets still reflects the vision for policing in a democracy.

Police Leadership Training

Building a team to carry out both democratic goals and crime-reduction objectives requires training. Police training in the past focused on upwardly mobile police officers, who essentially learned on the job from their senior departmental mentors. There was little external leadership training and limited contact by police leaders with members of the political, social, and economic communities. Most officers training focused on the legal requirements of the United States Constitution and its relationship to procedural law, rather than skills to handle the challenging human dilemmas that line officers face daily on the streets. Leadership training focused primarily on managerial skills and did not provide chiefs with the vision, organizational understanding, or motivational tools to achieve the goals of policing in a democracy.

Even though Vollmer recognized the great value of police training in the early 1920s, it continued to be constrained by time and organizational creativity. With only limited success in subsequent years, in the 1990s the U.S. Congress mandated a new effort at police training with the development of the national Police Corps. This training program highlighted the value of a college education and incorporated much of the discipline and physical rigor of the military. More fundamentally, the Police Corps focused on preparing police officers for actual scenarios they would confront daily on the streets of local communities. They were taught many of the lessons William Ker Muir offered in his book *Police: Streetcorner Politicians*, including the value of knowing how to talk with people in order to prevent issues from escalating into crime or other disorders.[12] Police Corps training was linked directly to developing police officers who could implement a community policing strategy in their assigned communities. It recognized that police officers are community leaders and provided them with the necessary skills to perform these roles. Though it focused primarily on new officer training, it also recognized the value of preparing future police leaders. In addition to Police Corps training, organizations such as the Police Executive Leadership Forum (PERF) initiated training at Harvard University that focused on leadership development. These two programs began to focus police leadership issues on a broader community context rather than a limited tactical leadership training, which had been the primary concern of past police leadership training.

Internal Police Culture

The police culture is a complicated territory. Police officers express a strong allegiance to their country, their community, and their fellow officers. Police officers expound a strong belief in respect for the law and respect for the values of their policing responsibilities. The culture is primarily focused on maintaining the customs and approaches of past policing methods and, in many instances, offers a limited level of support for many new policing initiatives. Long-time police officers are often reluctant to embrace new ways of working. Leaders who attempt to introduce change have to address behavioral norms firmly entrenched in the culture of the organization. Police chiefs who have been involved with community policing bemoan the difficulties of motivating their officers to accept a community-oriented approach. One chief described how his officers normally would retreat to headquarters on New Year's Eve as community members fired off their weapons to celebrate the New Year.

The code of silence is another difficult norm to overcome when attempting to get officers to give one another critical feedback and create more internal discipline. Obviously an internal culture that resists external critique or even internal feedback is not conducive to an honest, open review of organizational operations.

One of the leadership challenges after the Rodney King incident was the ability to manage the use of coercive force by officers. Few departments had ever established a personnel process that identified and corrected officer misbehavior prior to its being reflected by their negative actions in the community. The Ramparts Division scandal, which identified a tight-knit group of officers who engaged in drug theft and assaults on drug dealers in the Los Angeles Police Department, indicated that even positive values could be distorted. In the book *Official Negligence*, which describes the history of the LAPD, the description of the "cohesion" of the Ramparts Division units demonstrates how a valuable norm can become both dysfunctional and dangerous.[13]

In spite of the revelations about the Ramparts Division, Chief Bratton and others continue to address the challenge of reshaping their police cultures. In Los Angeles, Bratton talks about the power of the "warrior culture" in his department. Other chiefs discuss the difficulty of mobilizing the police culture to embrace and incorporate community policing. Police leaders want to empower their officers and the community, but, at the same time, they are responsible for ensuring the rights of people under the rule of law.

Police Unions

Since the 1970s, police unionization has matured into an important political constituency within the department, emphasizing the value and importance of the line officer. Unions have become the key advocates for police officers' benefits, work-related rules, and overall protection within the departmental internal affairs process. This has resulted in efforts to enhance and empower line officers within the department and within the community. In many states, the development of police unions has not occurred because of states' rights issues regarding workers' rights. The issue of officer empowerment continues to be a central theme for police leaders as they attempt to motivate their officers to meet the goals of the vision. There is some evidence of police empowerment in places such as Broken Arrow, Oklahoma, where the chief has been able to engage his line officers in developing new approaches to crime prevention and crime reduction.[14] In the case of Broken Arrow, the chief actively engaged his officers in the internal management of the department as well as the creation of specific new strategies to build a more community-oriented role for police in the local community. Still there are only limited examples of police leaders being able to muster the support of unions to actively participate in community policing approaches.

There is no doubt that chiefs must establish productive working relationships with unions, and, in most cases, this relationship revolves around wages, benefits, and matters of individual discipline. The broader policies of a police leader, however, are often either not confronted or not very clearly supported by the police union. Many of the chiefs interviewed for this study express their frustration with the continuing challenge to mobilize union support for their vision, especially if it involves a progressive focus on building strong community relationships.

Supervision and Internal Accountability

The manner in which chiefs manage issues of police conduct is critical to their success on the job. In recent years, police chiefs have made the issue of internal affairs and the maintenance of police integrity a primary focus of their administrations. In addition, many have developed new internal accountability structures to manage the daily performance of their officers. At PERF conferences in 2006 and 2007, as well as within informal networks, chiefs are talking about early warning systems, positive discipline–support schemes, improved data collection of officer performance, and new approaches to midlevel supervision and management support of officers. As police chiefs confront the issues of officer accountability and the impact of the police unions on the disciplinary process, they must still generate an active level of officers' participation in determining the allocation of resources.

External Relations and Political Challenges

Community Relationship Building

In the 1950s, the police chief stayed out of any overt involvement in politics and played a more technocratic role. Today's community-oriented policing approaches require an active involvement in the political life of the community. Many chiefs have found themselves carefully commenting on schools, health care systems, and local political issues that impact the police in the community. In Los Angeles, Chief Bratton faced a tenure fight for his position. He had established strong ties with a very diverse set of community leaders. However, during the tenure situation, Bratton also had to confront a serious set of misjudgments by some of his officers who violated a wide range of departmental policies when they mismanaged crowd control at a May 1, 2007, immigration rally in a Los Angeles park. Fortunately, Bratton's strong relationship with the community facilitated his reappointment for another 5-year term, in spite of renewed concern about the behavior of some of his line officers. Bratton's own reservations about the departmental culture remain quite strong.

Chiefs need to have strong political skills that enable them to integrate their mission with the overall goals of the community. One of the most critical ingredients of the police chief's role as a political manager is the ability to develop and maintain strategic relationships, partnerships, and alliances within the community. Bratton's behavior in Los Angeles demonstrates the necessity of developing these partnerships. Lee Brown, the former police chief of New York City, established some of the earliest community policing approaches in this country. He knew that his relationship with the community was important to his own tenure, but more fundamentally creating a new, productive style of policing in that city was a top priority.

Political Pressures

The impact of the external political world on the work and tenure of a police chief is powerful. The majority of police chiefs remain in their positions for an average of only 3 to 4 years. Those who are successful usually have managed to maintain a fine balance between their vision of policing and the demands of the politicians who put them in their jobs. Chiefs have faced demands by mayors to limit their community relationship–building activities in favor of stricter enforcement policies that have alienated portions of the community. Chiefs have also faced the challenge of their inability to appoint qualified candidates, as mayors have interfered with the chief's staff selection process. The police leader's role includes managing the strategies of law enforcement within the larger context of the politics of law enforcement. Recognizing this fine line seems to be a fundamental act of enlightenment, and how one performs the balancing act is the critical deciding factor in the success or failure of the chief.

Police chiefs struggle to balance their oversight roles within the police organization with monitoring from other political and community actors. James Q. Wilson says that mayors need to define the role of the police chief as "nonpolitical." In this case, the police chief operates as a managerial leader who has received support from the mayor. The chief attempts to operate outside of the political boundaries that might confront the mayor on a daily basis.[15] At the same time, police chiefs must educate their mayors about the past history of anticorruption-oriented policing in America. Chiefs must demonstrate their own clear commitment to law enforcement while mobilizing political support for their management of a first priority city agency. Again, it goes back to the chief's vision, which describes the police services that the police chief has made a commitment to deliver to the people of the community.

Accountability and Performance Measures

As police chiefs have struggled to establish their visions, they have faced numerous internal and external challenges to their management of police officers. Civilian structures for review of police conduct grew out of the need to challenge internal review processes as well as to provide greater police accountability and legitimacy to the community. Though police chiefs have used Compstat measures to monitor the department's efforts to reduce crime, there are limited tools available to measure individual officer street performance. In the absence of these officer measures and internal feedback processes to discuss problematic officer performance, external oversight boards have been established in some American cities. Applying external performance measurements to departmental goals further complicates police leaders' attempts to manage their departments and carry out their vision.

Police leaders have tried to establish indicators of police performance and accountability for over 50 years. In the 1950s, the key indicator of police leadership was the elimination of police corruption and the elimination of political involvement of police in external matters, such as elections or specific illegal business ventures. Managerial efficiency and commitment to technocratic goals were the primary measures of success.

In the 1960s, tense relations between the police and significant segments of the community were exposed and vilified. As the police institution attempted to respond to this negative exposure, police leaders established new accountability standards. For example, the chiefs measured response times to 911 calls and tried to demonstrate that these services had a direct impact on reducing crime. However, these measures raised significant questions about the impact and allocation of police resources, especially when studies such as the Kansas City Police Study found no evidence that the presence of police officers deterred crime in the city as a whole, even if it did in some high-presence neighborhoods.[16]

Police chiefs did their best to incorporate these research findings into new accountability criteria, which included both crime reduction and crime prevention. Although police departments had reported on Part One crimes (such as homicide and robbery) annually for years, the community policing approach provided a fundamental link to new strategies for preventing and allocating police resources to serious crimes as well as to lesser crimes in the community.

External oversight mechanisms, such as civilian review boards and other disciplinary processes, have a significant impact on police leadership. Whereas the value of participatory leadership is widely acknowledged, major political forces can and do present challenges, especially when a civilian review board raises questions about a chief's leadership in the department and the community. Questions remain whether a review board, which normally comprises citizens who monitor discipline or serious community incidents, can ultimately provide legitimacy for policing efforts and protect the rights of people in the community. This external process might be linked with an internal affairs disciplinary process managed through the police chief for the entire department. Oakland, California, and the New Jersey State Police are two police jurisdictions where police officers' accountability issues led to external federal monitoring. The focus in both jurisdictions was on racial profiling, police accountability, and allocation of police resources.

Private Security Services

In the past 20 years, there has been a significant increase in the use of private security services in many communities, which has triggered questions about how to reconcile the boundaries and costs of public and private security resources in a democratic society. The potential effect on public agency budgets is another challenge, as political, business, and community members evaluate police leadership and its effectiveness in providing security services.[17]

Significance of the Role of the Police Leader

The police organization operates in a world of great uncertainty, as reflected in the "situational discretion" of the line officer and the methods that police leaders offer to support the positive use of their authority. This underscores the necessity of managing the results of their interactions and providing clear documentation of the outcomes of the police services. Of course this organization of results has been another challenge that police leaders have faced in the last 50 years. Police chiefs have moved from measuring reduction of corruption, to documenting the reduction of serious community and police conflicts, to measuring their response to calls for services, and, finally, to the new challenges of documenting prevention of crime.

These are real challenges that police chiefs confront on a daily basis. Their vision is not a sterile guide to be followed blindly, but a template that reflects the values and the moral compass of both the police and the community. The police chief's vision is the focus of attention for the department, and a representation of the goals and vision of the entire community.

This study is designed to help the public understand how police chiefs operate in a democracy. Though the public expects the police to protect them, little has been written about how police leaders get this job done. With this in mind, 26 police leaders were willing to tell their stories about how they confront the serious challenges that sometimes make our communities unsafe. The police are the ones we call when we are in trouble and we expect them to do something about the problem after that call. The media tell us about the outcomes of police officers' responses to our calls. Now we will have the opportunity to meet these police leaders. Their stories will show us how police chiefs think, organize, and develop a well-functioning department that it is hoped will keep our communities safe and secure.

In today's post-9/11 society, police chiefs face many challenges, including shifting ethnic demographics, a rise in youth violence, and internal opposition to departmental strategies for law enforcement and community acceptance. Though these challenges are not necessarily new, they are complicated by organizational history and global developments. The police chief of the past, who only had to worry about the daily deployment of officers, is long gone. Today's chief is a community leader who must understand the balance between enforcing the law and ensuring strong community support for the police and their mission. This is the challenge that will be discussed in the following chapters.

Introducing the Police Chiefs

2

Profiles of the Police Chiefs

The 26 police chiefs interviewed for this book have unique stories to tell. They are a special breed because they have committed themselves to ensuring the safety of their communities while supporting the most important values of the United States Constitution. As this study unfolds, you will have the opportunity to meet people who have faced city councils, mayors, and, of course, some of this country's most dangerous criminals. Almost all of the chiefs started their careers as line police officers, but some of the most progressive police leaders bring experiences from other areas of community life. The field of police leadership is not a static, career-ending occupation, but may offer new opportunities for leadership in other community roles. One former chief now serves as a minister in a local community near where he served as a police chief. Others have "crossed the aisle" and have served as mayors or performed in other political leadership roles.

Former Baltimore Police Commissioner Leonard Hamm grew up in Baltimore and enjoyed a distinguished career as a police officer prior to his appointment as commissioner. He was a well-known youth basketball star who enjoyed great respect within the department and throughout the city. When he retired from department the first time, he next served as the director of school safety, first for the Baltimore schools and then at Morgan State University. After the mayor of Baltimore recognized the limitations of importing two New York City police commissioners, he enticed Hamm in the winter of 2004 to accept the position of Baltimore police commissioner.

Commissioner Hamm was a community-oriented, African American police leader who struggled daily with his own intuitive sense of managing the city's difficult social, educational, and economic challenges. He had intimate knowledge of a city school system that was failing and in disarray. He also knew the life of the streets well as a young man who grew up in Baltimore and as a police officer. Hamm had worked closely with two mayors who actively campaigned around issues of youth violence and homicide reduction. He also served as a police commissioner during hotly contested gubernatorial and mayoral elections. He was an optimistic leader who marshaled a committed following of line police officers within the department, as well as a dedicated team of top police executives who shared his mission for the department.

Hamm's observations about the life of the Baltimore police commissioner underscored the struggle of rebuilding a police department to meet the needs of a rapidly changing community. He epitomized the engaged urban professional with a regular-guy image that resonated well in a neighborhood-oriented city. Hamm also managed a zero-tolerance enforcement strategy while transitioning to a more community policing approach under a new mayor. Though Hamm was successful in many areas, the mayor, in the midst of a tightly contested election race, replaced Hamm. The primary election issue was crime. The homicide rate was rising and the Baltimore media pressured daily for a stronger police response. The mayor chose to bring in new leadership to meet that challenge or at least get the police leadership issue off the front page. Hamm's story is emblematic of the challenges other chiefs will discuss when they reflect on police leadership in a democracy and their communities.

In contrast, Commissioner Frank Straub in White Plains, New York, is an innovative, suburban police chief who has successfully navigated the political waters through two mayoral terms. He is the public safety commissioner, mandated to guide the collaboration of police and fire departments in support of major economic development in one of America's most prosperous cities outside of New York City. Straub's eclectic credentials include experience in the federal government, military, and urban police worlds. He also has a strong academic background, including a doctorate and extensive teaching experience, which enables him to carefully assess problems from an analytical as well as a practical point of view.

In the last 4 years, Straub's leadership has brought about a dramatic reduction of crime in the White Plains community, while supporting new initiatives designed to bolster relationships between police and youth to prevent the advent of gang violence. Straub is part of the new generation of police leaders who resolutely supported the use of Compstat to insure implementing the problem-solving approaches to crime prevention. He has found and applied new ways to develop supervisory personnel and addressed the rapid demographic changes in his community. Specifically, he has introduced a safe-housing plan, a youth violence prevention program, and numerous crime prevention initiatives designed to support a focused economic development program within the city. Although he is a thoughtful, reflective leader, Straub is known for his willingness to join his officers on bike patrol or climb ladders with his firefighters.

Chief Dean Esserman brought his New York City experience to Providence, Rhode Island, another challenging American city. Though he never worked as a line police officer, he had worked closely with some of America's most distinguished police leaders, including Lee Brown, William

Bratton, and George Kelling. Esserman got his start as an attorney with the New York City Transit Police. As general counsel and one of Bratton's key deputies, he provided hands-on leadership that reduced the incidence of quality-of-life violations, such as public intoxication and graffiti, in New York City's subway system. He subsequently became police chief in two Connecticut cities prior to his appointment to the Providence position.

Esserman was brought to Providence to reestablish police credibility in a city that had seen its dynamic mayor sent to prison for a wide range of corruption activities. He came in as a lone ranger forcefully and directly confronting the corruption within the police department. As a result of his efforts, he built a new institution committed to creating a reputation for integrity in policing. He has been described as one of America's preeminent police leaders. He is a strong advocate of community policing and has performed well as a member of the Police Executive Research Forum's inner circle of police reformers. Esserman has tackled some of his city's toughest challenges, including reducing youth violence and addressing serious internal police department corruption. He mobilized support both within the department and from members of the diverse Providence community.

Chief Ron Davis of East Palo Alto, California, is a new chief who worked for more than 20 years in Oakland prior to taking a leadership role in San Mateo County. East Palo Alto, a small ethnically diverse city near Stanford University, has seen its demographics shift dramatically from primarily African American to Latino and Samoan. Davis brings urban policing experience as well as direct involvement with federal consent decrees, where task forces are sent to cities in crisis to make specific changes in the police departments. He has assisted in reengineering departments with serious issues of racial discrimination, poor community relations, and uncontrolled use of force by police officers. Davis was brought to East Palo Alto by the mayor to build a professional department, and engage his officers and the community in building a diverse, economically viable, and safe community. His experience with the Oakland department taught him some positive lessons but also exposed him to methods of doing police business that were completely in conflict with his plans for East Palo Alto.

Other chiefs have had long tenures in a variety of departments. Robert Olson, who now serves as a special adviser to police services in Ireland, served as a chief in Minneapolis, Minnesota; Corpus Christi, Texas; New York City; and Yonkers, New York. While in Yonkers, he faced a serious set of internal challenges to his authority, including a mysterious incident where a bomb was found strapped to the chief's car at a local police station. He has extensive international experience and was the leader of an innovative community policing project in Jamaica that dramatically reduced the incidence of crime in several dangerous neighborhoods.

Olson's long experience is matched by William Lansdowne, the San Diego police chief, as well as Darrel Stephens of Charlotte, North Carolina. Both Lansdowne and Stephens have distinguished themselves as major proponents of problem-solving policing and have offered healthy critiques of the Compstat model of police accountability. Stephens is considered a dean of police leaders, as he provided innovative leadership that spawned the creation of the Police Executive Research Forum, the Washington, D.C., progressive think tank for police reform.

Although there are many distinguished long-time chiefs, Chris Magnus of Richmond, California, and Rick Fuentes of the New Jersey State Police represent a new generation of police leaders and offer important insights about police leadership in challenging policing environments. Magnus, a Caucasian, was brought from Fargo, North Dakota, to a predominantly African American city in California. He has confronted extensive internal challenges from a department that had essentially hunkered down and tried its best to withdraw from the community. Magnus directed that department back into a partnership-building approach with the community to address the high level of violence.

Fuentes was selected as superintendent of the New Jersey State Police soon after the department was slammed with a wide range of negative press accusations and a federal consent decree about their racial profiling policies. Though Fuentes had grown up in the department, he felt a strong commitment to rebuild the department's integrity and unravel its racial profiling practices in favor of a more community and racially sensitive approach to policing.

William Bratton, Lee Brown, George Hart, and Hubert Williams are some of the most engaging and committed police leaders in this country. Bratton has established a lifelong reputation for leadership and policing innovation. His tenure in New York City ensured him a place in the police leadership hall of fame. His creation of the CompStat model and the innovations that he brought to community policing are critical to the overall development of police leadership strategies in the United States and internationally. Bratton's book *Turnaround* documents his experience in Boston and New York City.[1] His interview helps us understand current police leadership challenges as well as new approaches that will guide policing in the future.

Brown has distinguished himself as both a police chief and a political leader. His interview outlines his reservations about the commitment of police leaders to the basic tenets of community policing and a vision that is inclusive of all members of the community. Brown was an early architect of the community policing approach. His skepticism about implementing this model is important to our understanding of police leaders' commitment to working with their local communities.

Hubert Williams—Newark, New Jersey, police chief in the 1960s and 1970s and now the president of the Police Foundation—expressed his concerns and hopes for the future of policing. Williams is a candid, sober assessor of past police experiences as well as a visionary about how the future of policing may evolve in this country. He was joined in his depiction of the history of policing by David Couper, police chief in Madison, Wisconsin, in the 1970s and 1980s. Couper lived through the student disturbances on college campuses. He tells stories about the tough challenges he faced both from the community and his department. He discusses his decisions managing police use of force and his respect for citizens' rights. Further, Couper collaborated with Herman Goldstein to develop problem-solving approaches to policing in the early 1990s.

Two Oakland, California, police chiefs describe their efforts to professionalize and modernize their departments. Hart, a distinguished police leader from the 1970s and 1980s, discusses his professional approach to policing as well as the challenges his colleague, Wayne Tucker, faced during his tenure in that city. Both Tucker and Hart have extensive professional criminal justice backgrounds and their stories describe many of the internal and external obstacles to community policing.

San Francisco Chief Heather Fong was an administrative executive in her department when the "Fajitagate" fiasco triggered the firing of five of the top commanders, including the chief. The scandal involved serious ethical violations by the senior police commanders and inappropriate use of force by two police officers. Fong was brought in to reestablish the code of ethics and integrity for the entire department. Her story shows the difficulty of implementing a politically mixed department vision, operating in a politically charged external environment, and attempting to build consensus within an unbelievably challenging internal departmental culture. The chief faced serious internal resistance from her officers and the police union.

Her other California colleagues are veterans, including William Kolender, who has served as San Diego County sheriff and the City of San Diego police chief as well as the director of the California Youth Authority. Joe McNamara, now a tenured teaching fellow at Stanford University, served as the San Jose police chief for 15 years and at 38 was the youngest police chief in America when he was appointed chief in Kansas City in 1973. McNamara is well known for his provocative media commentaries about police leadership. His interview was particularly engaging as he discussed the loneliness of the police leader within a changing police culture.

Richard Pennington, the current police chief of Atlanta, talked about his tenure in New Orleans, where he fired more than 350 police officers for corruption. Pennington has also served as an influential leader of the National Organization for Black Law Enforcement Executives. Another Atlanta chief, George Napper, was the only chief interviewed who had never been a law enforcement officer. He was a professor at Morehouse College when he got the call from Mayor Maynard Jackson entreating him to become Atlanta's police chief. The Atlanta police department was having serious internal and external struggles and needed a new type of leader. Napper had been a colleague of Lee Brown at the University of California's School of Criminology and was able to bring his unique academic perspective to the Atlanta Police Department.

Drew Diamond and Robert Lunney have been chiefs in major cities: Diamond in Tulsa, Oklahoma, and Lunney in Edmonton, Alberta. Both have had extensive experience promoting innovative, problem-solving methods and community policing approaches in the United States and other countries. Diamond is a leading advocate for community policing in the United States and has provided extensive consultation and support to police departments that have made commitments to rebuilding their police cultures and improving their relationships with local communities. Lunney is a well-known adviser to both American and international police chiefs, as he has a distinguished record for building strong, community-oriented police departments.

Another strong proponent of community policing is Gil Kerlikowske. He served as the deputy director of President Clinton's COPS program, which provided America's police departments 100,000 new police officers as well as many new programs and methods to support community policing. Kerlikowske now serves as Seattle's police chief and his tenure has been distinguished by rebuilding the integrity of the department after serious police failures during the World Trade Organization riots in 2000. Kerlikowske's observations about police leadership and the challenges of changing police cultures have been pivotal to the creation of a cadre of future police leaders.

Two police chiefs offer their experience with developing community policing and succession planning for police leaders. Ellen Hanson is a suburban police chief in Lenexa, Kansas. Hanson is a well-respected police leader who has established an excellent reputation for developing succession planning within her department. She has advised numerous chiefs on developing internal police leaders. She joins another fine chief, Jane Perlov, who brought community-oriented policing to Raleigh, North Carolina. Perlov was one of the first female commanders in the New York Police Department (NYPD). She was well respected because she had come up through the ranks. After leaving the NYPD, she served as the secretary of Public Safety in Massachusetts and then was recruited to Raleigh where she has served for more than 6 years. She recently took a position as a security executive for a major corporate banking institution. Another Southerner is the former chief of Hattiesburg, Mississippi, Charlie Sims. Sims served as a leader of the national Police Corps, a program created by Congress to establish new methods for recruit police training and police leadership development in this country. Sims has strong ideas about using training to challenge the status quo of the police culture.

Significance of Discussion: Why This Group of Police Leaders?

Many of the chiefs asked to participate in this study fostered some of the most significant reforms in American policing, including introducing the Compstat process and community policing. Others have successfully provided leadership in some of the most crime-ridden urban cities in the United States. Many have implemented innovative ideas concerning training and management. Still other chiefs have provided the critical leadership that assisted their city leaders in navigating the political and racial turmoil of the past 40 years. Many have a broad perspective from having served in several cities across the country.

Bratton, Brown, McNamara, and Couper will share their insights about the history of police leadership in the past 40 years. Other chiefs will discuss their personal experiences about promoting and leading change in their departments and their cities. All who participated are considered past, present, or future leaders of the policing establishment. They are a diverse group of men and women who have faced social, economic, and political challenges. Though not all started as police officers, they bring years of experience as problem solvers and mentors to other police officers, mayors, and community leaders, and they agreed to share both their positive and negative experiences. They discussed their mistakes, misunderstandings, and misjudgments as well as their successes. Their guidance and observations may assist future police chiefs as well as those who are interested in effective police leadership in their own communities.

A Vision for the Department and the Community

3

On February 10, 2007, a forum on police leadership was held at John Jay College in New York City. It was designed to promote educational opportunities for police leaders in New York State. John Timoney, the Miami police chief, was invited to give the keynote address. He was also joined on the panel by Providence, Rhode Island, Police Chief Dean Esserman; the former police chief of Rochester, New York, Dr. Cedric Alexander; Jeremy Travis, the president of John Jay University in New York City; and Dr. Maki Haberfeld, the director of the John Jay Police Science Program. Timoney was invited to discuss the challenges of police leadership in the United States.

At the outset of his presentation, Chief Timoney described the Knapp Commission era of the 1960s when the New York City Police Department (NYPD) was under intense scrutiny for its corrupt police practices. He had experienced this era of police corruption and the department's shift from an anticorruption emphasis to a focus on crime reduction. He discussed this reorientation of the NYPD's organizational strategy and then outlined some key lessons that he had learned as a police leader in New York City, Philadelphia, and Miami.

Recalling his Philadelphia tenure, Timoney lamented the lack of leadership, accountability, and buy-in from the police officers that underscored his negative experience in that city. There was no clear mission statement and the Philadelphia police culture was resistant to change. The civil service culture did not reward achievement, but quietly supported a negative, change-resistant, organizational culture. He described the police union as "one dimensional," with a system of personnel arbitration that included not only line officers but also his entire command structure. A union attorney at an arbitration hearing told one senior commander that "he should be careful with his statements against police officers as the same attorney may be defending him one day."

In his early Philadelphia days, Timoney had political and media support for introducing changes in the police department. Later, he found himself alone when the real challenges, such as reassigning incompetent staff and developing clear expectations for his line officers, had to be faced by the political leaders. He acknowledged that a major mistake had been his failure to fully appreciate the intransigence of the Philadelphia police culture. He then described the NYPD culture as being more supportive of change, innovation, and police officer education. He explained how the NYPD culture was well known for promoting police officer professional development.

In contrast, the Philadelphia culture was reluctant to encourage professional development and focused most of its attention on its internal civil service promotion structure. In the Philadelphia situation, Timoney lamented that the chief could only appoint one top command person outside of the civil service system. He felt strongly that his inability to appoint commanders for their talents and experience undermined his efforts to implement a progressive policing vision for Philadelphia.

Based on a more positive experience in Miami, Timoney stressed the importance of making changes early in one's tenure, remaining focused on sustaining the organizational changes, and building a culture that supports innovation. When he arrived in Miami, the first issue he faced was the excessive use of force by police officers. The departmental policy clearly prohibited officers from shooting at moving vehicles. Unfortunately, the norms of the department supported this practice in a variety of situations. Timoney enforced the policy of not shooting and clearly mandated that "unless there are tire tracks running over you" officers will not shoot at moving vehicles. He described how he implemented the policy change through active persuasion at all roll calls as officers went on duty. He also instituted significant changes in top management and continuously monitored every situation that involved the use of force. Through good communication and constantly reinforcing the policy, he established buy-in from his officers. This type of shooting is now rare, if nonexistent, in the department in Miami.

Another challenge for Timoney was establishing relationships with African Americans and Cubans after serious conflicts between the department and those communities. His role as a leader was to actively persuade his department and the community of the importance of community policing, problem solving, and respectful working relationships. This has been an ongoing challenge. From his perspective, the key to good leadership was building a team that would support his policing vision. In Philadelphia he had little opportunity for developing this vision or a management team. Fortunately, in Miami he had the latitude to do both as he could appoint a team of talented top commanders who supported his vision and the changes that he promoted for the Miami police department.

After Timoney's presentation, former Rochester, New York, Chief Cedric Alexander reiterated the observation that the consistency of the message from the top was pivotal to the success of a police leader. He also noted the balancing act police leaders face between internal norms regarding obedience to the chain of command and recently instituted norms that support police problem solving and police officer empowerment.

Chief Dean Esserman framed his rather subdued comments around a reference to the Greeks and Romans. He explained that the verb "to lead" in Greek carries the implication that the leader will die in the course of leadership.

He tied this analogy to the police leader's often lonely role and the difficulties of maintaining leadership in a city for an extended period of time.

Dr. Maki Haberfeld noted that concerns about police corruption in United States have been around for more than a century. From her perspective, it was only in the past 40 years, since New York City's Knapp Commission, that real efforts have been made to curtail police corruption. She suggested that training and education, as well as compensation for police officers, have been the pivotal elements of a new vision of police leadership that had helped create a more professional police force.

Timoney and his colleagues spent the evening describing many of the challenges police leaders face on a daily basis. Timoney's failure to understand the Philadelphia police culture prevented him from turning the department into a forward-thinking organization that would embrace his new approaches. Alexander described the difficulty of introducing strategies that require stiff enforcement of the law while insuring the mobilization of community support for police practices. Haberfeld's comments underscored the value of training, but also focused on issues of compensation and respect for the profession, especially when budgets are tight and cities struggle with how to measure the value of their police officers. Finally, Esserman candidly described the lonely role of the police chief who must contend with all of the problems of urban life while maintaining both internal and external support for the police department's vision. The John Jay forum on police leadership provided an exciting opportunity to hear police leaders discuss the challenges of police leadership in America. The stories offered in this study provide further insight into how chiefs manage many of these same struggles successfully and, in some cases, not so successfully.

Police Leadership in a Democracy: What Does This Mean?

The police chief is mandated to protect people's rights in accordance with the United States Constitution and ensure that officers perform their jobs within the requirements of the law. This basic legal framework is constantly drilled into the minds of police officers and its implementation is ultimately a fundamental mandate of police leaders. Ron Davis, the new police chief of East Palo Alto, California, is very cognizant of his role in a democracy.

> The role of a chief in a democracy is a simple question with a very complex answer. Historically, police chiefs and departments thought of themselves as enforcers of the law and didn't think they had much of a role in a democracy. Police officers at the lowest level of the organization have enormous power to make arrests, take freedom from individuals, and use coercive force. The police chief has to be able to manage this awesome responsibility so that the

officers are a part of the democracy and not opposing it. At the same time, the chiefs must balance the needs of the community and the political needs along with the issues of civil rights. My sense is that the police chief becomes really a facilitator in a balancing act. You have so many interests to balance, yet you still have to accomplish the basic law enforcement function of the police chief.

For example, you get competing interests in a community. Crime is up and they want you to be aggressive. But if the aggression becomes abuse, which is a likely case, then they worry about too much aggression. You have practical concerns about the officers doing the job out there every day, providing them with the resources and tools to get the job done. Then you have the political concerns, dealing with the city council and elected officials who also have to balance other city services against your needs and have to get reelected.

Even the enforcement of law is political by nature. There are some laws that are considered minor, so people don't want the police to address them. Still laws that are felonies do not allow for any discretion. Robbery is robbery, but enforcement codes and the potential aggressive enforcement of these laws can be problematic. There are other laws that can bite too because it's both a police chief's responsibility and it's also a public values discussion that can involve the community's political leadership. In that sense, the police chief should become the lead adviser, the lead technician, or expert to help guide the city council and elected officials in the right direction.

Chief Davis mentions others in the community that he must take into account when making decisions and choices.

Inside the department you have a balancing act with police officers, unions, and associations. Depending on the size of the organization, this can include rank and file and the police management. So you have to balance management, rank and file officers, political leadership, and the community. We say "community" as if it's one, but it's not. East Palo Alto, for example, has a very large Hispanic population, a large Pacific Islander group, and a large African American community, so this is primarily a community of color. You have to try and balance the needs of all those communities. You want to be consistent in the enforcement of the law, but you also want to tailor your delivery of the law, if that makes sense. If you don't balance that appropriately, it will result in disparate outcomes that could ultimately spell your demise as a police leader!

New Jersey State Police Superintendent Rick Fuentes sees the balancing act as having more of a national security focus.

There are probably two different definitions—before 9/11 and post 9/11. I've been a police chief for this organization in the post-9/11 era and there's now a blurred distinction between homeland and hometown security.

Both Davis and Fuentes clearly see the police chief as the key governmental leader, who must integrate the goals of a democracy through the political, community, and organizational structures in which they work.

Consistency of the Chief's Message

Chiefs who have successfully built strong, committed organizations all seem to be guided by a vision or mission statement. Of course, most books on leadership describe the value of a clear, focused vision for an organization, so it is no surprise that successful police leaders understand the value of their vision statement. The consistency of the message about the value of community partnerships and the importance of not alienating the community through "heavy-handed" police tactics were primary factors in former Commissioner Leonard Hamm's approach when he returned to the Baltimore Police Department after retirement.

> When I first came back what I had was essentially four different police departments with four different missions and four different messages. The reigning thought for officers was to make it through the day to save their asses. If that meant they had to backstab a brother officer, that's what they would do. I had to get everybody on the same page. I had to create one department again. In order to do that I had to make changes in personnel, changes in people, and those people that didn't want to abide by the vision had to go. There were some people that wanted to buy in to the new vision, some people that wanted to trust it. I had to create an atmosphere of trust and respect. I had to let these guys and gals who work very hard know that I trusted them. All I asked of them was to be honest with me, don't lie to me, and give me an honest effort, and we'll figure out the new direction together.

The organizational challenges Hamm faced after two successive police commissioners had been fired for lack of integrity had to be addressed by developing a new vision for the Baltimore Police Department.

Chief George Napper served as police chief in Atlanta from 1978–1982 and then as the commissioner from 1982–1990. He had never served as a police officer until appointed chief in 1978. His vision of the police chief in a democracy incorporates the concept of human dignity.

> The chief has to be very concerned about the human dignity of the people that he serves. I've always felt that a democracy had to be not only protected by the police, but also protected from the police in terms of the awesome power and authority they have, and the history of how they oftentimes have used it in a negative way. As a black police chief, I was mindful of that history and wanted to instill in all of our police and the various communities served a very strong

and meaningful understanding of what we would be doing as a police department. I had to ensure that human dignity was respected as a key component
of my vision for the department.

Napper was concerned about the response of his personnel when he presented his vision to them.

> I was aware that many in the police department were worried about being
> handcuffed themselves, as it were. I had the impression that they wanted to be
> able to do whatever they wanted to do any time they wanted to. I was very con-
> cerned about this kind of mentality, but there was never any kind of dilemma
> in my mind about the rights of citizens and the need to make sure these rights
> were protected!

Napper's close friend and mentor, Lee Brown, had a great influence on
Napper's tenure in Atlanta. A former mayor of Houston, Texas, Brown also
served as a police commissioner in New York City and police chief in Atlanta
and Houston. Brown is very clear about the need for a strong, consistent
vision and message for any police department.

> First of all, I believe in the concept of community policing. Community polic-
> ing is value-driven policing. All police agencies in a democracy must have a
> set of values that they follow and set rules by. Policies, procedures, training—
> everything a police agency does must be governed by values. One of the values
> must be that it's the role of the police officer to protect the constitutional rights
> of the people and that is just as important as enforcing the law. I see the role
> as probably one of the most important elements of government because their
> role is to protect the Constitution. If they do that, then in my estimation, they
> become the most important employees in city government.

As for the "balancing act" between protecting people's rights and enforcing the law, Brown observes:

> I don't think it's something that you balance. You are required by the nature
> of your duty to enforce the law. That's what you're responsible for. But you
> do so in the context of the Constitution of the United States and all that law
> results from it. I don't see any conflict. The Constitution is the overarching
> document that guides how police officers, and certainly the police chief, gov-
> ern themselves.

Brown then emphasized that the chief's vision sets the direction of
the department.

> The chief has to have a vision as to where he or she wants the department to
> go. I'm biased, again, as I believe in community policing. Once that vision is

determined, the chief must have the ability to articulate it so that the police department and the community understand it. Then the third responsibility of the police chief is to mobilize the members of his or her department as well as the community in implementing the vision. I think the important element for a police chief is to have a vision.

The Police Chief's Vision Provides the Balance for Success

Drew Diamond was the former Tulsa, Oklahoma, police chief and is now deputy director of the prestigious Police Executive Research Forum (PERF). He has been a consultant to police chiefs for many years and has developed an impressive record as a national and international police adviser who specializes in the problem-solving approach to policing. One of Diamond's and PERF's most challenging democratic policing successes was in Jamaica. Diamond and his team created a dramatic turnaround in a community that had been very undemocratic and crime ridden.

> Unfortunately, I've seen policing in nondemocratic settings, as well as seeing police violate democratic principles in our own country at times. In terms of police leadership, it is the chief's job to ensure that that police services in their communities, in the context of a democracy, are honest, play by the rules, are transparent to the community, and recognize flaws and are constantly trying to fix them. Democratic police forces have to be open and accountable. These are not clichés. This has to be built into the policies and practice. In this country and worldwide, police leadership sometimes thinks that their first priority, in terms of their own survival, is to take care of the needs of the men and women of the police department. That's not correct. The men and women of the department all raised their hands and volunteered. They know the risks. I want police officers to be treated respectfully and I want them to be safe. Still the first priority is the community. This is the balance that at times can be difficult.

Diamond again underscores the difficulty of this balancing act as he describes the variety of needs and interests that must be addressed by the chief. It is this ability to negotiate competing interests that many of the chiefs address, struggle with, and finally, if successful, learn how to manage.

Gil Kerlikowske, the chief of Seattle's police, has extensive police leadership experience as both a chief and as the former deputy director of the Department of Justice's COPS program. He has worked closely with chiefs in departments of all sizes throughout the country and sees a continuum in the way police chiefs visualize their roles.

Chiefs live and work within in a continuum. There are police chiefs who believe that it is solely their responsibility to run an efficient and effective law enforcement agency. Then at the other end of the continuum, there are chiefs who believe that their role is to pontificate on every possible issue from abortion protests to the death penalty. My view is that first and foremost you need to run a good police department. You can't be good on the outside dealing with the community unless you're good on the inside. If you have issues inside—corruption, professionalism, training, etcetera—you've got to take care of those things first. But you also have a secondary responsibility to provide advice and direction, policy, and guidance to the community on legitimate public safety issues that affect the people you're sworn to protect. Policymakers want that advice. You should do it in a reasonable, evidence-based way rather than off the top of your head. Your word in the community carries a great deal of weight.

The chief must have the officers understand that there are limits to their authority. These limits are established to protect people and, in some cases, even people whom the officers arrest. The other fact is that we are a nation and a community of laws. As upset and unhappy as they [the officers] may be at times with a court ruling or a change in the law, it actually strikes a good balance.

Kerlikowske focused on ensuring that the internal culture of the department was clear about its mission and its capacity to deliver police services in accordance with this vision.

Robert Lunney, former police chief of Edmonton and a few other Canadian cities, as well as one of the PERF's most knowledgeable consultants, has done a tremendous amount of work with leadership development. He was a key assessor of the Congressionally funded Police Corps program, which developed training for future police leaders. He was an architect of PERF's successful community policing program in Jamaica and has also worked extensively in Ireland and other British Commonwealth countries. His international work provides another perspective on the balancing act concept.

The role of the police is to support democratic principles and the chief is the one who best embodies them and insures that the force operates on those principles. I see it as a commitment to public service and I see the role of the police as balancing freedom and order. The question is how much freedom and how much order. These are the critical decisions to be made by any chief as he shapes the culture of his organization and the way he presides over its performance. The police are part of the social contract between the government and the people, and the people and each other. The chief's major role is order maintenance and law enforcement, but it's broader than that. At a higher level, I always thought of policing as social engineering. That gets us into areas of prevention and support for those positive forces in the community.

To carry out their roles, good police leaders need to have leadership characteristics. Chief Esserman of Providence, Rhode Island, outlined what he thought those characteristics might be.

> One is to provide public safety for the community, which is very different from simply leading the police department. My job is to manage resources of those under my command and those around me to work toward public safety. I look at public safety not only as being about crime but also fear, and I try to address both. I think the second role for me is to develop a Hippocratic oath for those that wear my uniform, which starts with doing no harm. The police have a history of doing a tremendous amount of harm and being apart from the communities. They have enormous power and a tradition of abusing it and they have a hard time reining it in. That has been for the most part the spark for civil unrest in this country—some sort of interaction between a citizen and a police officer. Sometimes one was at fault and sometimes the other. I've always believed that the greatest protector of civil rights could be the police because the police can enforce social justice.

Another reform-minded chief is Chris Magnus of Richmond, California, who served as chief in Fargo, North Dakota, prior to his appointment to Richmond. Although Fargo and Richmond have very different geographies as well as social and ethnic demographics, he focuses on the relationship between the community and the police, and whether the community gets "what it may desire or deserve."

> My vision is to have a department that really helps create a city that you can feel safe in and that you can enjoy living in. When you get people talking and engaged and really thinking about the city's potential, it always comes back to that vision and transforming the community into that kind of place. Departments have mission statements and visions that talk about quality service and professionalism and treating the public with respect and all these kinds of things. Don't get me wrong; I think all of that is extremely important. I look at those as maintenance goals.

Challenges to the Leader's Vision: External and Internal Pressures

When Magnus first came to Richmond, California, his officers were resistant to any organizational changes that required greater contact with the citizens of the community. Many were opposed to the very concept of community policing and engaging the people of the community in crime prevention. In addition, the crime rate was skyrocketing with a significant increase in the number of murders and shootings. The entire community was adamant that the new chief must bring dramatic changes in policing to the city immediately. He was well aware that his appointment was specifically linked to the community's commitment to change.

> In a lot of ways, it comes back to the notion that every community to some extent gets the kind of policing that they ultimately want and that they're asking for, even without necessarily thinking in that particular way. I was going to say what they deserve, but maybe that's a little harsh. Police departments really do reflect what a community wants. Sometimes a community's not sure what it wants and that also comes through very clearly in the type of police department it has. When a police department is under fire or subject to a great deal of public criticism, sometimes it says at least as much if not more about the community itself as it does about the department, in terms of how things have gotten where they are and what the community has gotten from its officers and from its chief. It says a lot about how neighborhoods have evolved in that community and what sort of things have been ignored or tolerated as well as encouraged and even nurtured. Although there certainly are some dysfunctional police departments, the great thing about a democracy is that this is what the community has allowed to develop. When a community's ready for that to change, I think then we will see real change in these departments where there is dysfunction.

Clearly Magnus is focused on safety and actively engaging the community in working with his department to achieve this goal. He knows well that this approach to crime reduction is as risky as it is potentially successful. His vision has been well received in the community, but in some cases challenged in the department. Still he has held firm to its implementation. The vision is an expression of the chief's and the department's values, although there may be conflicts between enforcement of the law and respect for the rights of people in the community.

Baltimore's Commissioner Hamm confronted such a situation, centering on whether the police should be focused on zero-tolerance enforcement for all laws or be more selective in their patterns of enforcement. There was strong resistance from the community to the zero-tolerance approach, especially the enforcement of loitering or drinking a can of beer outside of your home. Accordingly, he tried to balance community interests with the overall interests of law enforcement. Unfortunately, the politics of a mayoral election undermined his efforts and he was replaced by a mayor who was unwilling to confront the political pressures required to meet the challenges of a more community-oriented policing strategy.

Business writers describe the importance of the leader's vision and the failures of companies that lack a clear direction. Police chiefs also have a responsibility to articulate their vision to their officers and the community. Sometimes competing interests within both the department and the community cloud the vision. Many police chiefs have failed, as Timoney did in

Philadelphia when he was unable to provide a vision that resonated with and was inclusive of his police officers. Other chiefs have struggled with determining priorities for their departments and have been criticized by their officers and the people in the community for a lack of clear direction. Offering a dynamic vision is no easy task, but the recognition of this responsibility is fundamental to the role of the police leader.

The late Chief George Hansen of Lincoln, Nebraska, had a reputation for using modern policing approaches in the 1960s–70s when constructive relationships between police departments and their communities were becoming part of the police reform dialogue. Hansen's "Statement of Mission" shows his clear vision for that relationship.

> It is a cardinal principle of democratic societies that ultimate responsibility for peace, good order, and law observance rest with the community of citizens of that society, not with an organized police force.
>
> Although the very complexity of modern societies usually dictates that policing efforts be coordinated and directed by a force of paid professionals, their responsibility is derivative. Their role is to supplement and aid community efforts, not supplant them. And the power permitted to these police must be carefully defined and limited.
>
> A community which abandons its basic duty to police itself, to a professional police service, will soon find that the police can hope to provide no more than a bare modicum of public order and security and this only through such repressive measures that the basic liberties of a free people are eroded, and the very democracy that the police seek to preserve is endangered. Only if the proper balance is maintained between the basic responsibility of the community and the derivative responsibility of the police can a safe and order society be preserved with the least burden on individual rights and freedom.
>
> It is unfortunate, therefore, that the history of urban policing in America in the twentieth century is a consistent record of efforts by the police service to assume a disproportionate share of responsibility for maintaining social control, and the recurrent abandonment by American communities of their portion of the duty. The result has been an increasing lawlessness, which even increasingly repressive measures have been able to curb. The delicate balance between traditional roles of the community and the police needs to be restored. Peacekeeping must again become a joint police–community effort to stand any reasonable chance for lasting success.

Hansen outlined this vision in the early 1950s. He was well aware of the serious dilemma that police leaders would face if they were not able to build a strong, collaborative relationship with their communities. The observations that he outlines in this statement underscore the balance that police leaders have attempted to reconcile between their policing responsibilities and the peacekeeping role in the community.

Significance of the Vision of the Police Leader

The police chiefs discussed their views about the importance of a vision for their departments and their communities. In some cases, they talked about how a total lack of vision caused complicated, internal departmental conflict. The police officers were not clear about their mission and the departments lacked a clear direction. In Philadelphia, Chief Timoney failed to penetrate the police culture and establish an internal vision for the department. However, he came to Miami with a strong, clear vision about reducing gun violence and building support for the police in both the Hispanic and African American communities. Timoney worked energetically to communicate it to his department and the community. Other chiefs describe similar circumstances that highlight the importance of presenting a vision for the department and ensuring that the chief is well aware of the responsibility to constantly sell this vision to officers and the community.

The chief's vision also recognizes departmental and community values. In the case of the police officers, these values are measured carefully in conjunction with the overarching commitment to uphold the United States Constitution. The chiefs discuss this responsibility to these fundamental laws and describe how they try to balance the challenge of their enforcement practices against the framework of the Constitution. This balancing act never ends, but their vision provides the critical lens through which they make judgments about their police officers' actions in the community.

In the interview with Drew Diamond, he was asked about the importance of the chief's vision for the department. He reaffirmed the critical value of the vision and suggested two departments' visions that he had worked with during the past years. He provided the visions for both the Pasadena and San Rafael, California, police departments as clear examples of invaluable statements that provide the overarching guidance for the departments in their work with the community. The visions statements read as follows:

> The Pasadena Police Department will be a world class agency based upon a foundation of public trust, and dedicated to keeping the public in public safety.
>
> The department will serve as a beacon of excellence and innovation as we come forward to the 21st century.
>
> By fostering an atmosphere of partnership, we will embody a shared purpose with our community and our employees.
>
> We are committed to excellence developed through pride, setting the standard, and earning a reputation for providing effective, caring, and courteous service.
>
> We will capitalize on our strengths as a diverse community and work force to make this vision a reality.
>
> The San Rafael Police Department will be known for its community service orientation, its effectiveness at preventing crime through community involvement, and for providing a safe living and working environment.

Our enforcement actions will be based on respect for individual rights as well as our commitment to protect the safety of all persons within our community.

We will strive for professionalism and integrity by maintaining high ethical and performance standards. Our policies and procedures will be designed to give simple, clear guidance to all personnel. We will encourage and support technological advances along with training and professional skill development to enhance our effectiveness at fighting crime. The Department will remain committed to a cooperative team effort between all divisions. We will encourage and provide support for employees to be proactive and flexible in identifying problems and solutions within the Department and the community we serve.

Finally, police chiefs need to actively persuade others to dedicate themselves to the vision of the department. They must also give feedback to those officers who are not fulfilling their commitment to the department's vision. However, it is equally important to acknowledge the police officers' contributions and positive behavior in the community, a key component that it is easy to forget. Strategies and efforts to gather support for the vision from the local communities are another major challenge. The chiefs have identified many difficult external political challenges within the local environment. In the following chapters, the chiefs will describe these challenges of implementing the vision with an equal amount of passion and clarity.

Implementing the Vision

How Chiefs Make It a Reality

4

Joe McNamara tells a story about his first days on the job as the youngest police chief in America, replacing a very well-known chief who had been appointed the director of the Federal Bureau of Investigation by President Nixon. It was 1973 and the country was still in turmoil about the Vietnam War and civil rights struggles. McNamara was immediately confronted with a police shooting that occurred only 6 days after he arrived in Kansas City. A young African American man was killed by a police officer, and the circumstances were suspiciously unclear. The Kansas City African American community was incensed and demanded that the new chief address the issue of police brutality. McNamara met with his command staff and presented his plan to attend the funeral to show support for the young man. All of the commanders except the one minority member of the command team insisted that he should not go. McNamara listened to their arguments, but he felt strongly that he needed to demonstrate to the community that he understood the situation and supported fair treatment of all citizens. Because he decided to attend the funeral, he faced constant opposition by his commanders and his officers for the remainder of his 3-year tenure in Kansas City.

McNamara spent the next 15 years in San Jose, California, as one of the nations most innovative and respected police leaders and strongest proponents of community policing. He was on the cutting edge of developing new productive relationships between the police and local communities, based on his experience with the urban riots in the late 1960s. McNamara was also a chief who was committed to building relationships with diverse communities. Though he had this vision in Kansas City, he was never able to implement it because of the strong internal and external resistance to his inclusive approach to policing. When he came to San Jose, he was able to mobilize support for an "inclusive community" vision that resonated in the community and ultimately in the San Jose Police Department.

As chiefs describe their visions, they are also considering the leadership skills required for implementation. Most started with integrity and vision. Others noted the ability to establish good relationships with their own personnel and the community. Still others mentioned understanding the culture of the department and mobilizing support for innovative, community-oriented approaches.

Richard Pennington in Atlanta has a great deal of experience with the issue of police integrity. During his tenure in New Orleans in the 1990s, he was a well-known reformer who addressed some of the most serious internal police corruption practices of the past 50 years. He brought in the FBI to assist him and ultimately fired more than 350 officers. He offers these observations about integrity.

> I think integrity is number one. People have to view you as being of the highest integrity and that comes from the community and also from your own police personnel. Both have to trust what you're saying as being truthful and upfront. If they feel as though they cannot trust you by what you say or what you do, you won't be a very effective leader. I think your men and women need to be the same way in how they conduct themselves in the community and in the department.

Pennington's comments emphasized the importance of the leader's ability to walk the walk as well as talk the talk. He understands that the chief must be a role model for both the officers and the community. He believes that integrity and leadership need to start at the top of the organization. Pennington is also familiar with departments where a chief has had difficulty with either the community or line personnel.

> I've seen many people become police chiefs that don't make it. I've seen them come and go because the perception of them in the community was that they weren't honest or trustworthy or of the highest integrity.

Pennington addressed the issue of integrity straight on and rebuilt the New Orleans department from the ground up. He brought in the FBI to identify corrupt officers and focused on major changes in the police culture. He specifically outlawed the practice of police officers holding a second job in the local New Orleans clubs and bars, as this was a key ingredient that fed the corrupt practices of police officers. He was not well loved by some of the police officers, but the community welcomed his fresh, honest approach to building a police department that had reestablished the value of police integrity. Unfortunately, the results of his efforts to clean up corruption were marginalized after his departure, particularly during the Hurricane Katrina disaster. The New Orleans police department returned to many of its past practices after Pennington's departure. The leadership of the department basically refused to sustain his vision for the department and its constructive relationship with the community.

William Bratton, now the Los Angeles police chief, is well known for introducing the broken windows theory of policing. His work in the New York Transit Authority coupled with his work as the New York Police Department commissioner highlight his willingness to demand police accountability and focus carefully on a results-oriented form of problem-solving policing. Bratton offers this view about police leadership:

> It's really a combination of roles; there's no one role. One, a police chief is an innovator. There's an expectation, particularly in the new era of terrorism, that police will be more creative and innovative than they were in the 1970s, 1980s, and 1990s. Number two, the chief must serve as a role model. Three, the chief must be an optimist. In order to be a leader, you need to possess and exhibit optimism. The idea of looking at a crisis as a challenge is important. To paraphrase Gandhi, to create change you must become the change. You have to embody the idea that the role of the police chief is one of creating, nurturing, guiding, shaping, and changing organizations.

Diagnosis of the Problems: A Primary Task of the Chief

When Bratton and Jack Maple developed Compstat, they revolutionized both the police accountability systems and the overall image of government agencies. They publicly offered specific goals and clearly outlined strategies to provide crime reduction results to the community. Bratton considers an analytical approach to problem solving as another critical skill of a police leader.

> One of the things a leader has to be very good at is diagnosing the patient [in this case a city]. Boston, New York, and Los Angeles were three totally different cities, or three totally different patients. As a leader, you have to know the problems you're dealing with and the resources that you have to bring to the issues. You have to have a system, if you will, to maximize the resources that you have to bear on the problems that you've identified. I always like to use medical terminology. New York was very different in many respects than Los Angeles, although the results were the same. A lot of dead people, a lot of people shot in a city that was basically strangling on crime. This was the situation when I got to New York City. New York City's gang problems were very different than Los Angeles. Los Angeles had a lot of very small neighborhood gangs fueled by drugs. New York is a smaller, vertical city and more densely populated than Los Angeles. It also had a lot more medicine to apply to the problems. I had 38,000 cops in New York. The average precinct in New York is 3 square miles with 300 cops assigned. My average Los Angeles precinct is 40 square miles with 300 cops assigned. So I've got a lot less medicine for many more patients. I have to put my generic beliefs, skills, and tools in my toolbox and decide how to apply them and in what priority and what sequence? A leader has to be a good diagnostician.

Bratton is well known for his ability to turn around organizations that are looking for a new vision, and ultimately an improved relationship between the police and the community. He is particularly interested in staff development and has mentored a number of rising stars who are now top commanders.

Bratton's strategies in Los Angeles included decentralizing the command structure, and building strong accountability and officer empowerment at all levels of the department. He also had to reverse an entrenched departmental attitude that excluded the community from problem solving in favor of the idea that the Los Angeles Police Department (LAPD) would take care of everything on its own and in its own way. This approach was described by one of Bratton's top commanders as a "warrior mentality." The department was worried about the possible risks of sharing decision making, fearing liability for any mistakes. Bratton describes his approach to mobilizing support as follows:

> A successful leader is first somebody that's going to set goals that even he or she is going to be measured by. Those goals have a significant amount of risk involved in them. You can't be fearful of risk; you basically have to be risk focused. With those goals, you have to work with your senior management and direct reports to set up strategies to meet these goals. As you move further down the food chain, you create an environment where your captains and lieutenants have empowered your people with tactics that focus on strategies and focus on meeting the goals of the organization. That's where the inclusion component comes in. You include as many people as possible in the thought process about how we meet the goals of the department and then you hold them accountable for the power you give away.

Bratton clearly has generated a great deal of success with his leadership approaches in New York City and Los Angeles. Still, in Los Angeles, the police culture continues to resist some of his innovative ideas about the relationship between the community and the LAPD. At a rally to support immigration reform in May 2007, the leadership structure fell apart, and his elite officers attacked a group of demonstrators. Fortunately, Bratton's relationship with community leaders and his quick response in reprimanding the responsible police leaders allowed him to reduce the level of community anger and ensure the renewal of his contract with the mayor of Los Angeles for another 5 years. Following this turn of events, Bratton recommitted himself to changing the "warrior" police culture and building new collaborative relationships between his police officers and members of the Latino and other Los Angeles ethnic communities. He has received strong support from the mayor and the Police Commission for his leadership and vision for the Los Angeles department.

This situation clearly indicated that Bratton's community policing vision had not been institutionalized within all divisions of the LAPD. To his credit, he decisively recognized the problem, recommitted to his vision, and immediately gave feedback in the form of discipline to both his leadership team and his line officers. Though Bratton is one of America's leading champions of community policing, this incident clearly demonstrates that implementing the vision is a never-ending task of the police leader.

Active Persuasion: Gathering Support for the Vision

Building support within the leadership of the police department is critical to building the consensus for the department's vision. Bill Lansdowne, the veteran San Diego police chief and former chief of San Jose, shares Bratton's view about being a diagnostician for a department and city.

> You need insight. You need to be able to look at issues and problems and really make a determination as to whether these are the ones that are going to be fatal to you as a chief. The politics that will play out with these issues is central to this analysis. You need to be an extremely good judge of people. The legacy that the chief will leave behind is very important, including the promotions you make because that's the next generation of leaders. You've got to be careful to make sure you've got the right people in the right places, people with a commitment to service and who don't mind working hard. I always look for the person who volunteers for the job. On the positions that you assign, you have to be careful.

Lansdowne is cognizant of the fact that chiefs have to be able to sell their ideas.

> Chiefs need a skill that a lot of people don't have. It's not enough to be able to tell folks what to do; you've got to be able to sell the idea. You've got to be able to persuade them to meet the goals of the mission.

San Diego had a serious police officer retention problem. The solution depended on Lansdowne's ability to sell the city council on new salary increases for his police officers. To encourage his officers to remain, he applied a large dose of optimism, telling them he was making progress because a year ago the mayor had declared there would be no salary increases and now there was going to be a salary survey. Lansdowne thought that the salary survey agreement with the mayor set a new direction that would ultimately provide the data and support for police officer salary increases in San Diego. Lansdowne described how he approached his officers as a salesman of a vision that not only impacted the city but the police officers delivering the service. He felt strongly that the salary increase was necessary and would improve the department's officer-retention rate.

> For big cities to survive, you have to offer comparable salaries or more because it's stressful to go out there [in the streets]. You've got to be able to sell them [in

this case, the officers]. The only way you can do that is to build a one-on-one relationship. You've got to stand in front of them and get close enough to touch them so they feel a part of the resolution of the problem.

Robert Olson has been a police chief in three American cities and was also the lead consultant on numerous international projects, including PERF's community policing project in Jamaica. Now a senior consultant for the Irish police oversight agency, he describes a mistake he made in his first experience as a police chief.

When I took over my first department as chief, I had all the right academics and latest operational techniques packed in my carpetbag. But I neglected to start slowly by educating and collaborating with the people who were going to carry out these new operational ideas to gain their buy-in and sense of ownership. I foolishly thought that they would see the brilliance of this initiative and follow me to the devil's gate. When I got there, I was all alone. It takes time to change culture in our business and being autocratic will never get the job done.

Olson explained what he learned about empowerment, and engaging and persuading others to follow his vision.

In my next life, I formed several groups of personnel from all levels of the organization, gave them a vision of what I wanted to accomplish, and then empowered them and turned them loose on the idea. What came back, with a little shepherding, was a plan that was bought into by the rank and file and successful. It took longer, with lots of education within and outside the organization, but it worked. Patience is a virtue.

Police Leadership: It Can Be a Lonely Job

Seattle's Police Chief Gil Kerlikowske understands the limitations as well as the challenges of being a police chief.

For a chief there are clear limits to your authority as to what you can do, and not just legal limits, but also realities of policing unions, civil service, ordinances, and other officials. You have to recognize that you're not going to run the organization by fiat alone. Accepting the fact that you and your family are very much in the public eye and being aware of that. You've lost your privacy. Also you have to recognize your own strengths and weaknesses. If you're a big picture, visionary person, you better make sure that you have the detail people that are actually going to put that vision into place. Part of this reflection is the recognition the research shows that the biggest leap is from officer to sergeant, but I'd say that the biggest leap is going from whatever level you hold in the organization to the chief. Pat

Murphy [Kerlikowske's mentor and the former commissioner of the New York Police Department] once said to me that I could be the first deputy commissioner of the NYPD. It's not the same as being the chief of police because everything stops with you. You are the decider in all things. Recognizing and understanding this reality is critical and if you're not willing to accept the long hours and hard work and a thick skin for criticism, then you'd better think about doing something else and not accepting a chief's job.

Chief Dean Esserman knows that being a leader can often be lonely and requires strong values and determination. He entered a challenging postcorruption political environment in Providence, Rhode Island, that required great integrity.

Leading is having a vision of where you're going and a good history from where you came. I think if one doesn't have a strong vision and a strong set of values, then one gets distracted by the everyday inbox, the crises that occur, and the movements and fashions of the moment. So they are ultimately distracted from getting to the promised land that you need to believe in. I also think that leadership is often lonely, so if you're looking for a popularity contest and you don't know how to be comfortable in your own skin with your own set of values, then one gets distracted and wavers. Leadership is knowing how to put a foot in your organization and the other foot out of it. I think you have to be a strong believer in democracy and be a part of the community and not apart from it. You have to know how to lead your organization and you lead officers from the heart.

Esserman was able to engineer a significant turnaround in both the ethical and operational reputation of his department by building a strong relationship between his department and the community. He reorganized the departmental infrastructure so that it became well respected for its integrity and commitment to reform.

Chief Ellen Hanson of Lenexa, Kansas, is considered one of the leading proponents of professional development for future police leaders. The demographics of her community were changing dramatically, along with the economic environment. As a result, her police department was facing a decrease in available resources to address the new challenges that were presented by these changes. Her staff had little experience with diversity and change. However, Hanson was confident she had the leadership qualities and experience to meet those challenges.

I think you have to be absolutely honest and you have to be forthright and you have to be able to make a tough decision. You have to be willing to listen, not only to both points of view but every point of view! We really have to be

accountable to so many different interests and types of people and organizations as well as our boss and of course to our internal constituency. I think you
have to really be flexible when it comes to style but absolutely dead centered
when it comes to values.

Hanson's observations about incorporating different interests within the
organization and the community are essential challenges of a police leader.

American communities are changing dramatically socially and economically, so in many cases, the past practices may not apply. The 1970s
were a period of rapid social change and political upheaval. David Couper
is a minister now, but was the police chief of Madison, Wisconsin, during
the Vietnam War era. He had tenure under Wisconsin law, which meant he
could only be dismissed for a criminal act or violation of the law. However,
he faced a great deal of internal resistance as well as a tremendous amount
of criticism within the community for his efforts to maintain peace in one
of America's largest university communities. He still remembers the high
level of opposition among students, police, community leaders, and citizens
against the Vietnam War, and the many protest marches that took place in
Madison. His own assistant chief, a local sheriff, and other governmental
leaders demanded a more aggressive approach in dealing with student demonstrations, whereas his response to the protest marches was to "keep the
peace, not just keep the streets."

Couper describes the turning point in developing his approach to keeping the peace on the streets:

> I got some special training for a number of young officers who agreed that it
> was foolish to beat people up all the time. We put together a special operations
> group of police who would be involved as conflict managers and who I gave
> a large amount of latitude to keep the peace. It turned the corner for us. The
> conflict on the streets was reduced and we stopped beating the students.

Couper was a close associate of Herman Goldstein, one of the principal
architects of the problem-solving policing approach developed in the 1990s.[1]
This new approach focused on identifying the problem and developing a
comprehensive, prevention-oriented solution to correct the problem. This
was a new concept for police officers, as they were accustomed to responding
to problems only after they had become crimes. Couper introduced this new
prevention strategy using a leadership style that allowed for feedback, role
modeling, and active persuasion of the officers. He constantly went out into
the streets to ensure that he was actively engaged with his officers as they
interacted with the community to solve problems. He outlines his approach
as follows:

I was never a police command officer until I was chief. What I strongly believed came to light when my daughter graduated from Officers' Training School in Georgia and her platoon motto was "Lead from the front." I always worked on the street in uniform, at least once a month every summer. I went out and checked systems, I worked detox [drug and alcohol detoxification facilities], I went to ER [hospital emergency rooms], and I went to places where cops hung out and got feedback, good and bad, about how the department was doing. I believed strongly in that way of doing business. When they [the cops] said I was asking for too much restraint from them and they saw me getting provoked on the streets like anybody else, I had to start practicing what I was preaching.

Couper used the media and public forums to make sure his vision of peace on the streets was communicated both to his officers and the community.

Many times a police leader cannot actively persuade people to follow the new path. In these cases, he or she may have to change the organizational culture and bring in new people to support and implement the vision. A leader must be able to understand when it is necessary to make these changes and, most important, how to implement effective change within the organization. Frank Straub, the Public Safety commissioner in White Plains, New York, talks about the importance of buy-in to bring about change.

Getting people to buy in to something new and separate from doing the same thing the same way for 30 years was a challenge. Getting them to embrace change was the challenge. Getting people that were obstructionists out of the way or out of the department was another challenge. [In Straub's case, he elevated some junior leaders to significant command positions and demoted commanders who refused to participate positively and actively in promoting his department's vision for the community.] Identifying leaders within your organization at multiple levels who bought into the direction that you were going in and that were willing to commit and take risks is another challenge. This is something that had never been done before in this department. Those are probably the most essential things that we faced in the beginning and those are the things that made us successful over time.

Straub has been able to bring the White Plains police and fire functions together in an integrated Public Safety Department, one of few in the country. He has also reduced crime statistics significantly while building a new culture of policing in a suburban edge city. Other police leaders have recognized Straub for his integrity and innovative approaches to policing.

Police chiefs are cognizant of the fact that the average tenure of a police chief is less than 4 years. Success or failure depends on having a clear and consistent vision, as well as good relationships within the department and outside with the community. An understanding of the police culture and the ability to lead and promote the vision for the department are clearly essential characteristics of a successful police leader. Chiefs also talk about the lonely nature of the job and the tough decisions that must be made to ensure that implementing their vision meets the needs of the community and supports their officers. The next chapter will look at enforcement strategies and the primary role that the police and their communities play in those efforts.

Significance of Implementing the Vision

The chiefs described the lessons they learned about the importance and value of persuading others to support their visions. Chief Olson discussed the length of time that it might take to build consensus for the vision. He talked about educating his officers so they would understand, support, and ultimately implement the department's vision. He describes how he rushed the implementation of his goals in one department and failed to mobilize support of his officers. Bratton's recent failure to realize complete support for his community-oriented vision only underscores the reality that the selling of the vision never ends. Changing the police culture could take many years and is not an overnight assignment.

All of the chiefs subscribe to the basic tenet that the vision is essential to building a strong organization. Business leaders and commentators also recognize vision as the central ingredient for creating a strong, successful organization. Engaging the department officers and the community in a shared vision is an outcome that police chiefs work diligently to achieve, but it is never easy. There are clearly different implementation strategies, and the reality is that some are successful and others are not. Some chiefs, including Lee Brown, used a strategic planning process to engage all of his commanders in the development of his department's vision. Bill Lansdowne discussed his "open door" strategy, which enabled him to discuss the department's vision informally with officers at every level of the organization. Finally, Commissioner Hamm implemented a community-wide goal-setting process, which enabled him to mobilize support from both his officers and the community for his department's vision.

Innovation and accountability for performance are additional tenets that support the vision. Chief Bratton discussed introducing accountability for officer performance through Compstat and individual performance management systems as a central characteristic of his police leadership vision. Other chiefs discussed the importance of engaging or even empowering the officers to make certain their commitment to the vision's implementation in the community. Some chiefs described the internal resistance from their own officers that undermined achievement of their vision in their communities. They realized that the implementation strategies are as important as the vision itself.

Police leaders can evaluate and ultimately impact their police cultures. All of the chiefs interviewed for this book faced serious issues within their organizational cultures. Chief Pennington faced rampant police corruption within the New Orleans Police Department. Brown was brought to Houston to instill a new relationship between the department and a rather distant community. All had to analyze and understand the norms of their departmental culture. These norms were not the rules but, more significantly, the way that the police actually did business. They were the realities the chief had to face if there was going to be real change in the department and its relationship with the community. Some of the chiefs have successfully changed the norms and implemented new strategies that foster a close, productive working relationship with the community. Others have struggled to change norms and failed to establish their vision both within the department and the community. It is the understanding of the linkages between the vision, the culture, and the norms that ultimately assists any leader to plot an implementation strategy enabling the organizational vision to become a reality.

Strategies for Enforcement and Working with Communities

5

The riots in American cities in the 1960s and 1970s forced police leaders to examine their departments' relationships with the community. National commissions, local media, and police chiefs' direct experience pointed to the distrust and fear many people felt for the nation's police.[1] As a result, police leaders began to experiment with ways to build and improve relationships between the police and community. The United States Congress developed a set of educational incentives that supported a federally financed, college-level program designed to recruit future leaders into the field of policing. Studies of police practices indicated that the seemingly tried-and-true strategy of random patrol of neighborhoods was virtually ineffective in preventing crime.[2] In addition, the total reliance on the 911 call system began to fall out of favor with police departments as departments responded to calls but made little impact on preventing crime. As a result of these realizations, police chiefs like William Bratton began to explore new accountability methods to manage resources and prevent crime. The Compstat accountability strategy was introduced, and it carefully managed and monitored police managers' allocation of police resources as well as their development of targeted strategies to reduce crime. In other words, the processes and strategies for reducing crime were as important as the outcomes. Developing supportive community partnerships was also one of the cornerstones of these new police strategies. However, police leaders still struggled to visualize what community collaboration would really look like.

Community Policing and Police Accountability

Police leaders sometimes face resistance from their officers when they try to introduce positive collaboration and partnerships between the police and the community to prevent and solve crimes and other community problems. Providence Chief Dean Esserman traces the evolution of community policing.

> More than anything, it's a reaction to what was. It's really a story of a post-modern era and post-WWII America. It's a story of a police world that was caught up in a trend of enforcing laws and thus changed the name to law enforcement. We went from foot to car and from car radio to waist radio. We gave America 911 [call-for-service system] and told them to call the police and

51

our job was to come. We became report takers and very sophisticated apologists who could explain why we couldn't do anything about the crime. We found importance by centralizing our power and our way of delivering services. Community policing was first and foremost a reaction to that response mentality. We had set up all of these report cards [about our ability to reduce crime] and we had failed miserably. Second, something was going on outside the police department, which was an enormous takeoff in crime and fear, and a pandemonium that became politicized in the 1980s. Then in the 1990s, it became a central political conversation that cut across all of the country's elections. Crime became the primary national political issue. I remember talking to so many mayors over those years that didn't know what community policing was and didn't care. Research told them that their citizens were dissatisfied and this approach sounded good, so they imposed it on police chiefs who didn't know what it was either.

The police did what they always do, which is to give the public what it wants; they would create a community policing unit and this would get the public off their backs. Rarely did they understand that it was a philosophical change. First, community policing means that you need to listen to the community. Partnership with the community is where the problems will be identified and where solutions lie. It was really trying to think about how to really value prevention when you only receive medals for apprehension after the fact. The goal was to take Herman Goldstein's beliefs about problem solving and replace what was a strategy of just addressing the symptoms, not the real problems. In the community, there has been an absolute demand for change in policing approaches. Community policing was born in the 1990s and is being now birthed in 17,000 different communities. It was a very difficult cultural change for the police, and a very different type of relationship had to be established with the community.

At the same time, police chiefs were also establishing new accountability structures to ensure that crime reduction and community satisfaction could be measured and resources allocated to meet these twin objectives. Esserman talked about the institution of the Compstat accountability model for measuring, tracking, and holding the police internally and externally accountable for achieving the goals expressed in their organizational visions and missions.

Compstat was not just a management tool; the police were going to be held accountable for crime prevention and reduction itself. They would stand up, whether in front of a television or the community or their own people, and say we are accountable. Crime going up is our failure and crime going down is our success. We had come off a generation of police leaders who simply would not accept that. There was a sequence of events that set the context for this approach. Politically, there was the desire for accountability. We decided to imprison as many Americans as we could to reduce crime. The economy was getting stronger. But there was no question that the police were doing something that they had never done before. They said hold us accountable. And that's what we do here in Providence now.

The broken windows theory developed by George Kelling and James Q. Wilson identifies new strategies for addressing deteriorating neighborhoods.[3] This idea suggests that the following sequence of events can be expected in deteriorating neighborhoods. Evidence of decay, such as accumulating trash and broken windows, that remains in a neighborhood for a long time provides evidence that people living in this area feel vulnerable and begin to withdraw. They become less willing to intervene in public order or to address the physical signs of neighborhood deterioration. The police have used this strategy to develop new approaches that target a wide range of activities to prevent an increase in crime in these vulnerable neighborhoods. Police have used the Compstat data analysis process to target specific enforcement strategies as well as nonenforcement approaches to clean up neighborhood areas overrun by broken windows deterioration and the increase of criminal activity.

Police have found that their own inclination to focus on homicide rates might not be the local community's primary concern. In fact, police leaders now talk more about issues such as trash, kids on the corners, broken-down cars, and a wide range of irritants that people in the neighborhood use to measure the quality of their police service.

Many chiefs, including Richard Pennington in Atlanta, have found that one of their primary challenges involves managing the pressure to saturate an area with large numbers of police to reduce crime without alienating the community.

The number one thing I've learned from addressing the quality of life issues, including Compstat, is that there has to be a delicate balance. By that, I mean that you want officers to work for you, but you don't want them to become so aggressive that they start to violate an individual's civil liberties or rights. There's a quota you have to bring in so many bodies every day, and these officers start thinking that they have to go out and "get some meat to bring to the table" because if they don't supervisors are going to be looking for them. So who cares if they lock a guy up and don't have probable cause, because if it gets to court they'll throw it out anyway. So what I learned from New Orleans and my experience with Jack Maple is that when you put that kind of pressure on them, many officers will start to fudge the numbers and pick people up for inappropriate things. You don't want these officers under so much pressure to enforce broken windows or start to do a great job for you and you don't have a way to monitor what they're doing. The numbers and stats may go up, but your excessive force, brutality, and complaints will go up with it.

Pennington's experience was shared by Commissioner Leonard Hamm in Baltimore. As he organized the establishment of a strong, new community policing approach in partnership with local district community councils, Hamm was also challenged by an enforcement-only mind-set that permeated the political and internal police culture. There were a high number of arrests due to the pressure for arrests first, but there were also serious charges from members of the community about the overly aggressive behavior of his police officers. Meanwhile, the state's attorney could not support the high number of arrests by the police department, complaining that the documenting of the arrests was inadequate. The lack of support for the strong enforcement methods created a crisis of confidence in the police from the community's point of view as well as from that of other governmental partners. Hamm adjusted the zero-tolerance approach in favor of closer working relationships with the community, but he had great difficulty selling this approach to some political leaders. In Hamm's case, the mayor wanted to implement a "strict law enforcement" policy that essentially gave the police direction to make a large number of arrests for even the most insignificant illegal activity such as sitting on your porch with an open beer container. Hamm also faced internal challenges as commanders and supervisors unrelentingly produced high arrest numbers that seemingly indicated a reduction in crime. Hamm talked about rebuilding the support from the community as pivotal to his community policing approach in Baltimore. Hamm used the targeted Compstat data model for targeting enforcement, but he coupled his approach with a focused community relationship building campaign.

> The community loves this approach because we explain what we want to do before we do it. If the majority of the neighborhood says they don't want it, we don't go in. We've got to have the neighborhood buy in. Now every place that we've gone, the neighbors have bought in to our approach and curiously we have been able to improve the level of safety and security in the neighborhood. I believe that they've maintained this support because now they have pride in their neighborhood because someone in city is showing them some hope.

Hamm worked hard to redirect his department away from an arrest-only or zero-tolerance strategy and toward engaging the community in a partnership with the department. At the same time, he was well aware of the need for successful management of the balancing act between accountability and a problem-solving approach.

The challenges of community policing and changes in police culture are often tied to the availability of police resources, as Chief Bratton illustrates in Los Angeles.

George Kelling describes Los Angeles policing as "stranger policing." One of the reasons there seems to be such a comparison, particularly between the African American community and our police department, is that with so few police we have traditionally focused on more serious crime. Since so much of that serious crime is in our poor and minority neighborhoods, it has created a tension. But the style of policing here is very assertive and very police-officer-safety conscious. Because we have so few police, there's no time to develop the relationship with the community. My idea is to expand the LAPD so that there are other officers. Even though they may still be assertive because there's so much crime in neighborhoods, they will get some more time to develop intimacy and awareness of what that community wants in addition to dealing with major crime. For example, in the south side of the city, they want abandoned cars, crazy dogs running around loose, and gang-related graffiti dealt with. These are things I could address if I had more resources.

Bratton has a strong vision of community policing, but is also focused on enforcement. One of his primary challenges is to reorient a police department with a long history of operating exclusively within its own culture. His department is still evolving from Chief William Parker's era in the early 1950s, when police professionalism and maintaining distance from the community were supposed to insure a corruption-free department. The history of LAPD's community relations has been stained periodically by serious negative encounters, which have bred decades of suspicion and made the tenets and values of community policing that much harder to introduce. Still Bratton has worked hard to develop communication and bridges between the police and the community.

We had the professional model of policing, then we went into the problem-solving period, and then problem solving was embraced under community policing, with an emphasis on prevention, partnership, and problem solving. The 21st century terminology would be intelligence-led policing. This is linked with the Compstat concept and its four principles: gathering timely and accurate intelligence, responding to that intelligence, effective tactics for what intelligence is telling us, and then relentless follow-up. The underlying principle for Compstat, which was the big change linked with community policing in the 1990s, was accountability. The police were accountable for something. The major change in policing from the '70s to the 21st century is moving from a total response focus to a proactive, prevention focus.

The 21st century has brought the risks and challenges of terrorism to police departments, in addition to gang- and juvenile-related crime and an increase in youth violence. Bratton, like other chiefs, uses technological innovations, including cameras and data intelligence systems, to monitor and refocus the use of force. Still he continues to support community policing and the relationship between police and the community as critical indicators of his department's success.

Community Policing or Can You Arrest
Your Way Out of Crime?

Lee Brown is considered one of the primary architects of the community policing model. He came to Houston, Texas, as an outsider and quickly led his management team through a strategic planning exercise that primarily focused on a department's relationship to the community.

> I think it's very simple. One of the roles of the police is to control crime, but the police can't do it alone. That's been proven over and over again. By the same token, the community can't do it alone either. If you add the two together, you have a force that can make a difference. The police need the eyes and ears of the public in order to prevent crime. They need information from the public in order to solve crimes. Without the cooperation of the public, the police would be inefficient.

Brown gave examples of how his officers met regularly with community residents to discuss specific crime issues. His officers also worked closely with residents on specific problems to reduce burglaries and juvenile crime issues. When asked about strategies of strict law enforcement and the power of arrest, Brown replied, "I don't think you can arrest your way out of crime. You have to deal with the problems that create crime." He acknowledges the value of arresting those who break the law in some circumstances, but he also attests to the need for problem solving to prevent arrests from being necessary in all cases. A problem-solving approach is pivotal to mobilizing community support.

Drew Diamond, a longtime colleague of Brown's and a former Tulsa, Oklahoma, police chief, is one of the principal problem-solving consultants for the Police Executive Research Forum (PERF). He offers this wonderful example of "what problem solving means to the police" when he describes his work with his city's elderly population:

> Community policing has always been the context in which I have applied the tools and techniques of collaborative problem solving. As the chief of police in Tulsa, Oklahoma, during the late 1980s, I was faced with a large segment of our elderly residents who feared for their safety. Their fear came on the heels of two unconnected homicides in which both victims were homebound elderly. Even though both cases were quickly resolved with the arrests of suspects, the fear remained. At this time the usual police response would have been a

combination of just telling our elderly residents that the threat was over and that the police department would remain vigilant. We, the police, would then be ready to move on to the next crime. The difference for me was that my sense of community policing led me to think in a more holistic way about both the safety and quality life for the elderly in our community. I did not have to do this alone because at this point I was fully engaged with other social service stakeholders dealing with health, mental health, and social justice issues. Taking a problem-solving approach to the issue required, first, a scanning of the situation the elderly community faced. This scanning resulted in identifying the problem for the elderly not as one of potential crime victims but one of their increasing isolation from the mainstream of their community. The second step was to do the analysis around the problem of the isolation of the elderly. Working with both police data and social service data a picture emerged of the lifestyle of many elderly, particularly those that were homebound or somehow disabled. This picture showed that although there were good community services available and for the most part being delivered, the sense of isolation was real. Response, the third problem solving step, resulted from our problem-solving stakeholders' team developing a multifaceted approach that engaged police officers, social workers, and neighbors in an effort to both increase protection and inclusiveness for their elderly neighbors. I felt a key to this effort was to provide emergency responders and social workers a means in which they could not only know where the most vulnerable elderly resided but sufficient background information on their situation so they would be able to make appropriate response decisions and be proactive in protecting them. I offered to have this information entered into the police and fire 911 communications system. To accomplish this goal, the problem-solving team had to develop a simple form for the elderly to fill out and a mechanism to get the form distributed along with the technical aspects of data entry into the communication system. Initially, I was told that no one would voluntarily put personal contact information, medical information, and residential living arrangement information into a police database. They were wrong; eventually thousands of the elderly citizens provided their personal information. Concurrent with this effort, we assigned teams of beat police officers and social workers to go door to door in those neighborhoods where data showed a high concentration of homebound elderly (based on Meals on Wheels clients, Cohen nursing clients, and service providers input). This resulted in a higher level of awareness by the beat officers and neighbors of the elderly in their neighborhood that may need additional attention and support. It also became clear to potential predators that the interest of the police and neighbors in persons they might victimize had become more intense.

Diamond suggests that the assessment phase of his problem-solving effort during the first year of the activity showed a reduction in fear by the elderly and a significant reduction in actual crimes against them. This example of problem solving demonstrates the commitment of a police chief to work directly with members of the community. It also emphasizes the chief's understanding of the social value that police officers can offer the elderly community and ultimately all members of a neighborhood. Crime prevention may seem to be a less exotic form of police work, but the results of the prevention and problem-solving work can offer dramatic results that really impact people's lives.

Bratton was Brown's transit chief during his New York Police Department tenure as the police chief. At the time, he, too, was looking for new approaches to policing that would support accountability and solve problems. He started a data analysis project in New York's 72nd Precinct that focused the command staff on monthly data analysis and computerized crime-data reporting, a prevention method that Bratton took a step further. As Brown explains:

> Bratton assigned [Jack] Maple to be his crime guy. They did something that I did not approve of, but seemingly they just beat up the commanders over their precinct management and the use of the crime data. This was the beginning of Bratton's Compstat method, which raised questions in my mind, but I still supported the experimentation with this method of accountability.

The Compstat method has strong supporters and some detractors. It brings police commanders and their staff into a weekly accountability session with the department's top executive staff. Each police commander receives a focused inquiry about crime patterns in his or her district during a specific period of time. The commanders must describe their crime-prevention tactics, their allocation of police resources, and the results of their work in the community. This is a "stand and deliver" performance for the commander and the local district police staff, which is generally highly stressful for commanders, as they are publicly held accountable for the performance of their officers' crime-prevention and crime-reduction efforts. These sessions are generally internal, though some chiefs have begun to invite community and other criminal justice agency representatives to attend. Though many chiefs have found the Compstat process to be a positive accountability measure, others express discomfort with the aggressive hammering applied in the process.

Darrel Stephens of Charlotte, North Carolina, is one of this country's most seasoned and respected police chiefs and one of the founders of the police think tank PERF. He was an early supporter of Herman Goldstein's problem-solving approach to dealing with crime.

> The police are responsible for creating the safest community they possibly can. A lot people—community and police—feel the best way to do that is through the criminal justice system. They believe that strong enforcement and additional beds in the prisons deters crime and makes everybody feel safe. The

trouble is that experience over the years has never really borne out that idea. So if you come in as a police chief and your idea is just to use enforcement and the criminal justice system, you're not building anything that has a lasting impact on creating safe neighborhoods and eventually you lose the trust of the people you need to be engaging with.

Our criminal justice system in North Carolina is totally broken. It's overwhelmed, underfunded, and we can't get cases prosecuted. In Mecklenburg County alone, there are 38 trial dates for property crime offenders and we arrest thousands of them. They'll file about 75% of the cases, but most of them are working their way toward a plea deal. It's an important piece, but you need to focus on repeat offenders. I think there's clear evidence and clear research that if you get the most prolific offenders and incapacitate them, jail is a good way to deal with them. But that doesn't deal with all of the other issues that are out there, such as fear.

Fear is not always connected to the amount of crime in the community. There are a lot of other things that contribute to fear, such as traffic. Traffic is a big deal to people and their sense of safety in a community. You've got to have effective enforcement and criminal response, but equally important to all of those things, you have to somehow help people coproduce safe environments. In many cases, crime can be prevented by people changing their behavior in ways that aren't very complicated. People can unilaterally decrease their own chances of victimization and this can reduce crime, too.

Stephens' vision for the Charlotte–Mecklenburg Police Department is to "create the safest community that we can." However, he admits that it is not easy.

The most difficult part of achieving this vision is working with the people inside the department and those in the community, and helping them see that there has to be balance to achieve a safe community. You can't rely on just the prevention aspect through work in the community and you can't only rely on just the enforcement aspect. It is a balance.

Many chiefs talk about involving their officers in problem solving, but have questions about how to empower officers to actually implement that approach. Chief Stephens tells the following story:

Just a few years ago, we had an officer who had been on the street maybe a year in an area not too far from downtown. He had responded to two or three burglary calls at a cookie factory. They were stealing stuff out of the trucks and then actually getting into the factory and stealing from there. It was a factory that had basically let its security lapse entirely. The officer remembered that we did training in crime prevention through environmental design. He didn't have the training yet, but he knew what "Step Ahead" [the title of this training component] was, based on his academy and field-training experience. Rather than take the burglary reports and let somebody else deal with it, he contacted somebody in his division who had taken the training. He worked midnights but met the other officer in the daytime along with the manager of the plant. They walked through and did a good evaluation of their security, using lighting and accommodation fencing and changed a couple of internal procedures. They implemented these measures. They haven't had a burglary that I know of since then.

Stephens has publicly questioned some of the aggressive enforcement approaches generated through the use of Compstat and the broken windows theory. He's a very strong proponent of the problem-solving approach to policing, but well aware of the limits in changing organizational police cultures to meet the objectives of a crime-prevention orientation.

What was really on my wish list was a police department that had a much better idea of the best way to create a partnership for a safe community. Most police departments will have 5, 10, or 20% of their folks who really know community policing and problem solving and are engaged and enjoy it. What I want is a department that can handle calls effectively, do good criminal investigations, and do quality work in arresting people, but most importantly, a department with people who look at problems and think, this has happened, but how do I prevent it from happening again? What do I need to know? What do I need to understand to help change that environment? We've got a substantial number of people who respond to things in a different way than most police departments that I've worked with.

Stephens feels that there is a danger that Compstat stresses enforcement and arrests to the detriment of prevention.

There's a strong pull toward just being a friend of the criminal justice system. There's a belief supported by a lot of people in the community that the most effective police departments are the ones arresting the most people. They believe that there's a real deterrence from the threat of arrest and if you just had enough cops and other things, you could lock up enough people to make a safe environment. I see this attitude coming back.

My problem with Compstat is that it seems to focus on enforcement and leaves the prevention issues out of the discussion. What Compstat did was convince people that this was the best way to police. Just follow the statistics. If you have a bump there, flood them down and knock it down that week, then go somewhere else the next week and sort of chase it around. That's what we were doing when I started in the late '60s and '70s. This is short-term thinking. We don't get to a point where people are sharing responsibility for creating a safe community and the perception is that it's all a police problem only.

Stephens' observations challenge many enforcement strategies that have been linked with Compstat, intelligence-led policing, and the broken windows theory. Many chiefs support the Compstat model for its focus on resource allocation and establishment of an accountability norm that had been missing in the police culture. Stephens acknowledges the contributions of Compstat data gathering as it does support many problem-solving approaches.

> We get good real-time data. We do bring people together to talk about data and crime statistics and we have a task force that focuses on robberies and auto theft and enforcement activities regarding that. But that's basically 50 or 60 uniformed people in the department. We have a total of 1,200. So we're not ignoring our enforcement responsibility, but in addition to handling calls for service, we're trying to focus on understanding the problems and engaging people to resolve them. So when people say that's soft, it may be, but they've also come to understand that we don't have a criminal justice system that works, so we've got to look for alternative ways to try to change the environment.

Chief Stephens clearly feels he has made tremendous strides in the incorporation of the problem-solving approach into his department's policing strategies and culture. He is not an apologist for his critique of the use of Compstat, but recognizes both its value and its limitations in achieving short- and long-term policing goals.

Chris Magnus came to his present post in Richmond, California, after 7 years as police chief in Fargo, North Dakota. Richmond is a diverse city, which has been plagued by violence for many years. Magnus was brought in to build a partnership between the department and its neighborhoods to reduce violence and promote a safer, cleaner city. When asked whether reducing the homicide rate would be the measure of success for his tenure he replied:

> Yeah, but I think the climate in which people are committing homicides doesn't strike the guys who are doing this as such a big deal. When asked why they are doing this killing, their response is, because we can. They never think they can't get away with it in this neighborhood. What this tells me is that we have to change the climate and piece by piece take back the neighborhoods. We have to get citizens and the officers to get a sense of ownership that involves understanding the value of quality-of-life issues, broken windows issues, the misdemeanor arrests, the strategic ways to send a message to bad guys and the good guys even if we don't have the manpower at the levels we'd like.

Bringing the Police and Community Together: How It Can Work

Magnus talks about the value he believes the community policing approach offers in Richmond, California.

The reason I like working here is that my vision of community policing is a lot like what I think people in the community want. They want that sense of ownership on the part of the officer for the neighborhood. They want measurable progress on what they experience when they go out to the park or the bus stop. They want it to look and feel different than it does now. They want to feel as if their priorities in the neighborhood are our priorities for the department. This is a very diverse city and each neighborhood knows what it wants and needs from the police department. I want to have officers that know that and have developed effective partnerships with the community. If the focus has to be more on problem liquor stores in the neighborhood, then that's what the focus should be. If the neighborhood requires more attention on traffic, then that's where the police department should focus. It needs to mirror what it's going to take for people in that neighborhood to actually feel like this is a city that they want to live in.

Magnus inherited a department mired in its own call-taking and response-and-report-writing style of policing. He has been implementing organizational changes to meet these goals, including a new departmental decentralization plan. The geographic model was linked to a Compstat meeting for his officers and members of the local community. Magnus shifted the focus of his patrol officers from a citywide perspective to specific involvement in one of three local police districts. He wanted his officers to get to know their community, and for the community to know and hold his officers accountable for local issues. The response from the community to this locally aligned police resource was very positive. A number of calls indicated that people felt a stronger police presence and improved focus on neighborhood issues. Magnus designed a community policing approach that established a direct link between enforcement and the broken windows strategies. He has coupled this strategy with higher visibility and involvement of officers in the neighborhoods.

Down the road from Richmond is Oakland, whose police department was well known for the professional, community-oriented leadership of Charles Gain and George Hart. In the 1960s and early 1970s, Gain established a police culture of professionalism, a strict code of ethics and integrity, and a well-managed internal affairs department. Gain was also one of the country's first police chiefs to establish a significant relationship between the police department and the African American community. His deputy and active partner, Hart, inherited the department and served as its chief for almost 20 years. Though Hart was considered the model of a professional police manager during his tenure, the decade following his retirement left Oakland in a leadership vacuum.

In recent years, the Oakland police department has faced many allegations of misuse of police authority and inappropriate use of force by its officers. As a result, the department found itself operating under a federal consent decree, which mandated a group of outside monitors to provide rigorous, constant scrutiny of its policies and practices. The current Oakland police chief, Wayne Tucker, established a performance management system for his officers to ensure optimal supervision and early identification of officers' negative behavior patterns. The system was also designed to provide specific remedial action to improve an individual officer's performance on the street. Tucker discussed his approach to community policing.

> The broken windows theory and the zero tolerance idea have real merit. We can show examples in the city of being able to bring that off. We're actually damn good at enforcement of laws. What we don't do as well is the preventive aspect of the policing job. We've had problems with the mission of our department over the past 10 years and only focused on enforcement. We forgot that we need to work with children and families and actually eliminated those services within our department. This is an important part of our work. If we're going to make progress in this city, the police ought to be recruiting as well as the gangs do. We're looking at some strategies to work with our at-risk youth populations. We're trying to develop some new alternatives to crime reduction rather than enforcement only.

In addition to the federal mandates, Tucker must work with a city-appointed commission that has departmental oversight. He bemoans the fact that the culture of his department does not support community policing. A significant part of the difficulty has been the inability to resolve some organizational issues, including expectations of the community advisory board that police officers will take a problem-solving approach to crime prevention while also cutting down their response time to 911 calls. He is particularly concerned about the lack of clarity about what a community partnership should really look like to both the officers and the community.

> My staff gets really upset if a police officer identifies more with the community and residents on their beat than with the department. I've tried to tell them that's a measure of success. I can't do anything about it, but people worry about it. While it's a little irksome, it suggests that we're doing something right.

Chief Tucker has been actively promoting a series of initiatives to resolve the issues addressed in the federal consent decree, in the midst of the ascendancy of a new mayor and a departmental culture that has limited relationships with the community. He wants to promote a community policing model while maintaining such enforcement initiatives as the gang-focused violence reduction program titled Ceasefire. This program combines some aggressive enforcement strategies with prevention-oriented initiatives, including the introduction of social services for youth to facilitate withdrawal from the gang culture.

Ron Davis of East Palo Alto, California, previously served as an officer and commander in the Oakland Police Department as well as a member of the United States Department of Justice's Consent Order teams. As a result of this experience, he has clear views about the balance between strict enforcement and problem-solving approaches in the community.

> Without strong leadership, you can send your officers into the community and instruct them to be aggressive until you get the push back from the community. There are sensitivity issues, overzealousness on the part of officers, and citizen abuse. It all depends on how you send them out. If you send them out and allow them to "take the gloves off," saying we're going to kick butt and take everyone to jail, you'll have a problem. There are consequences to that.
>
> What I wanted to do when I came to East Palo Alto, a town primarily populated by people of color, with significant gang activity and poor police–community relationships, was demonstrate that the department could carry out the broken windows theory, which I do embrace. I wanted to be very aggressive on crime reduction without being abusive and actually start strengthening the relationship with the community at the same time. It doesn't have to be an either/or situation. We're starting to show that because our relationship has drastically improved; still at the same time we're into really strong enforcement.

Davis is quite proud of the positive new relationship between his department and the community. The department used to have very little communication or direct involvement with community members and organizations. One reason the department is more responsive now is that Davis divided the city into four beats, each of which has a sergeant and a team that holds regular monthly meetings in the community. Initially, the chief conducted the meetings, but now the sergeant facilitates them, and the response has been positive. The community is establishing its own relationship with its officers, who moved from a posture of aloofness to one of active community engagement and relationship building.

Davis also initiated a Compstat model that had not been previously used. The department had essentially organized its officers to randomly patrol East Palo Alto neighborhoods. Following Davis' appointment to East Palo Alto police chief, he used data to organize an effort to reduce graffiti, as well as to demonstrate to the community that his police officers could actually prevent crime. Clearly Davis has been able to parlay the positive and negative lessons from his Oakland experience into new opportunities for East Palo Alto.

One of the country's most distinguished police leaders is Hubert Williams, president of the Police Foundation. Williams was a prominent police leader in Newark, New Jersey, and well-respected colleague of the founder of the Police Foundation, Patrick Murphy. He describes some of the early police studies undertaken by the Police Foundation, including the Kansas City study, which was pivotal to the reevaluation of the use of patrol cars to deter crime. Studies also indicated that any positive interactions with police officers of a nonthreatening nature make people feel safer and improve the reputation of the police.

> The foundation of community policing is predicated upon this study's findings. Anytime I'm running a police department and I can improve the department's reputation and make people feel safer, that's a winning strategy. [However], community policing is in a state of evolution, as chiefs are still not talking the same language about the same things.

Williams notes that police often find it difficult to build relationships in the community, particularly because of race and culture issues.

> The [race] issue is not resolvable through generalities. You have to peel the layers off, so let's be specific about it. You have class differences and you have racial issues. We have not resolved the racial issue in America. You have White cops trying to go down and interact with a Black community and that's a major challenge. There are some White cops that do it effectively and develop respect in the community. Some come from a more integrated community or they have friends or relationships that cut across the cultural divide. But what happens when you start bringing in people who don't have any exposure to this stuff and they start to get uneasy, scared, and make really bad decisions and mistakes in terms of what they say and what they do. We do not know in this country how to communicate effectively across the racial divides. It's a huge problem that gets swept under the rug. I don't think you can have effective community policing unless you select and train officers to deal with cultural and racial diversity.

Williams called attention to the demographics of many communities that are recipients of the community policing, broken windows, and zero-tolerance strategies. In many cases, new police officers are recruited from suburban environments, with little cultural diversity or experience with inner-city, urban realities. Police leaders must then develop training programs that ensure officers are capable of showing respect and sensitivity, which is the framework of the community policing model.

Rick Fuentes has been dealing with a consent decree that arose from issues of racial profiling as well as concerns about the New Jersey State troopers' ability to work with people of color. He was appointed from the ranks following a series of negative experiences for minority citizens with the state troopers. He now works closely with other police leaders to establish improved internal performance-management programs. He says these systems support officers' efforts to work respectfully with members of all communities.

In some respects it boils down to making the community more active in the betterment of the community itself and not expect the police to do it alone. There has to be a certain landscape of law and order. If you have a lousy looking environment, which will translate into the health of the community and illegal activity may be the existing reality. The improvement that we've made to the environment as a result of broken windows helped on one hand, while on the other hand getting the officer out of the car and interacting with the community has worked, too. Operation Cease Fire, which is a gang interdiction and prevention strategy, is what we're instituting now. We're going to be introducing it in 20 cities, which will assist in reducing shootings in Newark and Irvington. There's a community outreach program that involves exerting pressure on "shooters" [people using weapons] as a community, because before the norm was to shoot first and then look around for witnesses. People would go inside after the shootings and not come out for 3 days. Now the community rallies against the shootings, which takes away that security blanket for the shooter. More than that, they go out and interview or make contact with police witnesses and coax them to come forward and talk with the police. This is a huge step forward.

Fuentes is a product of the state trooper culture and has experienced some of its most negative aspects. Still he is slowly building a new culture and vision in the department, focusing on a basic working relationship with community partners.

Frank Straub of White Plains, New York, describes how he approached enforcement in a new, downtown restaurant and bar district that has emerged as a central entertainment hub in Westchester County.

You can't just beat the heck out of the community; you have to explain what you're doing. Education and enforcement go hand in hand. The community has to agree that it's the right thing to do. When we do the downtown bar enforcement, it's really something that goes back and forth. Sometimes it's really strong and then there's push back from the bars or the business owners and then we have to back off a bit and change our tactics. Maybe we deploy resources differently or deploy different resources that are less offensive to the community. For example, we have a bar downtown that was the center of a lot of gang activity. It took a tremendous amount of police resources. We had heavy enforcement with uniform cops, horses, motorcycles, and plain-clothes officers. I would generally get out there too on Friday and Saturday nights, talking to people in and around the location to get a sense of what the impact of our tactics were on the community. People actually said they liked to come to White Plains because they know they're not going to get hurt by the police and appreciate the police presence. I was also watching the police and they were really engaging people well. They were talking respectfully; they were laughing, joking, and engaging people in conversation. It wasn't a bunch of robots moving people into cars or telling them they couldn't go in a particular direction.

In addition to the growth of the entertainment market in White Plains, Straub had to deal with a growing immigrant population. He has developed community outreach programs to improve awareness of safe-housing issues, and daily police-liaison work with the city's day-worker population. Many chiefs are developing new community-oriented programs to prevent crime in immigrant communities. Some have formed committees to keep the federal government from requiring an immigration enforcement function at the local level. Straub sees safe housing as one way to build relationships with the new immigrant community.

> It's amazing that the safe-housing task force hasn't been recognized as more controversial than it is. A number of communities in the metropolitan area have gotten into trouble by taking a very strict, regulatory approach to housing issues. We've taken a strong approach, but we're not looking to displace people. We've focused on making the housing safe and holding landlords accountable, which has resulted in fewer structural fires. We also make a concerted effort to engage the Hispanic population. We're all over the community in terms of domestic violence and have an innovative program to address these issues. We've also worked closely with the banks in town to get bank accounts for new immigrants so we can prevent robberies. It's a small thing, but key to our prevention strategies in this community. It's important to discuss personal safety habits with people. It's about building trust and educating people. It's important to show people from other countries that they can trust the police. The police can actually help you. It doesn't mean that we're not going to do our job, but we're also here to make sure that they can walk the streets safely.

Straub's efforts resulted in a 5-year record for crime reduction in his city, as well as a community policing approach that has been well received in all segments of the community. He has achieved this through education, communication, strong enforcement, and the development of tactics that work with the community.

There is continuing dialogue about the conflict between community relationship building and enforcement strategies of police departments. This discussion takes place within the ranks of police leaders as well as within the community. In many cases, chiefs face resistance from the community and other agencies when the enforcement strategies are too strong. The need for community support for crime reduction and prevention efforts is beautifully illustrated by a story from David Couper from Madison, Wisconsin.

> We're basically hierarchal, control-oriented organizations and it takes a lot of confidence to have police officers gain that kind of [community policing oriented] control. I remember one time when we had all of these people with

warrants coming into the police department surrendering to our officers. People were saying, "What the heck is going on?" Well, one of our neighborhood officers, a woman who knew almost everyone in the neighborhood, was given this warrant list. She said, "I can't grab these guys, but I know them, so I'm going to give them a call on the phone and tell them I have a warrant for them and they need to take care of it. I don't want to embarrass them or myself picking them up in the park while they're playing basketball." Most of the guys turned themselves in. Some of our officers said, "A warrant is a warrant and she can't do that." I said, "Well let's look at the end result. Do we trust you to do that?" I didn't take their complaints and it turned out to be a good strategy that I have to admit I never thought of. To me, community policing is flattening the organization and empowering police officers to get the job done creatively, if need be, and in line with the community.

Significance of the Police Department's Relationship with the Community

The debate over how to balance enforcement approaches and community partnership building is far from over. Some chiefs have integrated community policing into their department cultures, whereas others pay lip service to this idea. Some have decided that community policing is passé and believe the solution to the reduction of crime is greater use of intelligence gathered from and about the community. In many ways, all of these strategies require some kind of relationship with the community, but the form, depth, and level of the partnership remain an open question. In addition, the long trend of crime reduction seems to have slowed. Federal resources to promote community policing have been shifted to fund post-9/11 homeland security initiatives.[4] Still police chiefs recognize the value of community policing and problem-solving approaches to crime reduction. Sustaining and expanding these approaches will be a continuing challenge.

Police chiefs struggle with the notion of how to work with the community. Many have formulated a clear strategy for doing so with the community, but then must determine how to introduce this approach into their departments. Even after a community policing approach has been introduced, there can be a continuing struggle to convince police officers of the value of working closely with the community. Egon Bittner, one of the foremost police academics, wrote many years ago that more than 85% of police work is really analogous to the role of a community social worker.[5] Of course, the majority of police officers would reject this analogy or refuse to acknowledge publicly that being a police officer involves more than just catching "bad people." Still, they would have to acknowledge that communication training helps them deal more safely and effectively with sensitive and often dangerous domestic household calls.

Introducing accountability and planning methods such as Compstat has also been a challenge to police leaders. Compstat has enabled chiefs and their commanders to reexamine how they allocate their resources, and analyze the impact on community crime-reduction and crime-prevention strategies. Whereas many chiefs have welcomed introducing these methods, others are concerned that a top-down management style limits the potential empowerment of the line police officer. Chief Bratton is a strong proponent of the Compstat methodology, while Chief Stephens and others have expressed reservations. The major impact of this discussion has been a stronger sense of performance accountability for the department and, in some cases, for the individual officer. It is clear from the discussion with Chiefs Tucker and Fuentes that there is more work to be completed to ensure a stronger sense of individual officer accountability. Developing clear feedback processes and performance accountability for officers is a primary task for police chiefs. The tough issue with these newly designed processes is how to enable the community to have their own sense of how police accountability really works and how they ultimately can impact the relationship between the police and the local community.

Comments and examples about how community policing can really work are encouraging as they indicate a role for both the police and the community. Chiefs believe the debate is an important one and continue to look for evidence demonstrating the value of this critical collaboration. Perhaps even more encouraging are the police leaders' demonstrated willingness to listen and learn.

Developing a Professional Police Officer
It's a Challenge

6

In the mid-1990s, the United States Congress funded an innovative police training program called Police Corps. It was modeled after the Army ROTC program, offering young people a 4-year college education in exchange for a 4-year commitment to serve as an officer in a local police department. The Police Corps residential training program incorporated community policing theory, methods, and approaches into an innovative police training curriculum. During the design stage, hundreds of local police officers from around the United States were asked to identify key training priorities. Experienced officers responded that new officers needed to know how to talk with people and learn what to do with their hands. By this they meant officers needed to know how to defend themselves, but also how to present themselves to people in a less confrontational manner. This clearly reflected concerns about new officers' abilities to communicate with the public in a respectful manner. The Police Corps took on the challenge of training officers who would understand not only the theory behind community policing, but also the specific actions required to make the theory a reality. Many of the chiefs interviewed in this book have Police Corps graduates in their own departments.

A primary responsibility of the police chief is to oversee selecting, training, and motivating of their police officers. Though all chiefs recognize the importance of police officer development, there is still a debate whether policing is a profession or a craft. The majority of police chiefs have focused on developing a professional structure for police officers. Clearly, their efforts to establish selection and training programs to reinforce professionalism are still subject to great challenges. As departments have moved from a professional, technocratic, and exclusionary model to policing models that focus on developing a working partnership with the community, chiefs understand the need to recruit and develop a new breed of police officers. In many cases, they need to build a diverse workforce while continuing to build the morale of their officers. In addition, it is evident that the initial police officer training, at best, still teaches the basic police tactics without instituting an ongoing leadership development program that is similar to other professions. In addition, chiefs are still struggling with the meaning of a police officer working with people while maintaining their authority and a crime-deterrent presence in the community.

Chief Drew Diamond of Tulsa, Oklahoma, has thought about police training both as a chief and as a consultant in domestic and international police jurisdictions. He is a strong proponent of community policing and problem-solving models, and has definite views about the state of policing in America.

> We were fearful of being too close to the community and coming out of the corruption model of the early 20th century, so we chose the professional model. We did a good thing by becoming more professional, but we did a bad thing by thinking we had to remove ourselves from the community. The community didn't corrupt us, we corrupted ourselves. The idea is somehow the community will corrupt us, but I think it will ensure our professionalism. The goal of community policing is to make certain that we can work with the community rather than separate ourselves from it. Police training needs to reinforce these values and actually show new police recruits how to make this happen at the patrol level in our communities.

Gil Kerlikowske, Seattle chief and former deputy director of the Department of Justice's Community Policing office, points out that many chiefs find it difficult to recruit officers that live in their cities and also meet diversity goals to ensure the department reflects community demographics.

> Recruiting and diversity are huge issues. The question is about whether you are trying to mirror the community as best you can. Of course you have to work to make the public understand that it isn't really critical to have exactly 9.5% African Americans on the police force. In the same way, people ask, why can't we require that all officers live in the city? We have officers that aren't all that wonderfully accepted in the community and they live right here in town. We have other officers that commute from 30 miles outside the city and they do an absolutely wonderful job for the 9 hours they are here. Living in the city doesn't automatically guarantee that they're more invested in the city.
>
> It's just like we've shown in the days of rape investigations. We thought the only people who could investigate rapes were women detectives. The research tells me that a sensitive, caring man can actually be more effective than some women. In my mind, the same holds true for race. A White officer can do a darn good job in a Latino community. Out of all the big cities, I think Los Angeles was the only one that mirrored its community. I don't think anybody saw the community as incredibly engaged with that department or would describe the relationship as warm and fuzzy.

Kerlikowske looks at values, respect, and professional service when recruiting for his department. He has been a major supporter of leadership training that promotes community policing. Still, it is evident from Chief Diamond's and Chief Kerlikowske's comments that the relationship between the police and the community is still open to discussion. Though chiefs express the great value that a police officer can derive from a close working relationship with people in the communities, many chiefs are still contending with the basic issues of how to get police officers out of their cars and talking to people. In many cases, this vision and its values are not reinforced on a daily basis within the police organizational culture. Accordingly, the chiefs' vision of about the relationship between the community and the police gets lost in a crime suppression value, which reinforces the suspicion and distance from the community that many police officers carry onto their shifts.

Police Training and Its Link to Leadership

As the chairperson of the Police Executive Research Forum (PERF), William Bratton is a strong advocate for developing police leadership programs that ensure more active collaboration among police, other public agencies, and community leaders. He is critical of the disorganized way that police officers are trained and the resulting lack of leadership and professionalism.

> We as a profession have as one of our major tenets the development of future professionals and leaders. We do not have anything on the order of architects, engineers, doctors, or lawyers. We don't have schooling that brings police officers to a plateau where they have been educated to deal with all the issues they might face. Instead we take people from the lowest common denominator and grow them up through no organized system of education but a real hodgepodge of experiences, and hope that when they get to the level of chief their experiences have prepared them for what they are going to face. The reality is that within the police organization we don't teach how to deal with crime. Nobody teaches crime reduction in America today, unlike a doctor who is taught to perform surgery. We don't teach leadership. We teach management and supervision, but not leadership. A lot of what we rely on is technology, intelligence, computers, and forensics, but we don't teach people how to use it most effectively. We rely on the fact that as a detective you might have had a call in the crime lab. Even in community relations, we have no curriculum or certification. We don't have a license to practice as other professions do. The closest we've even come to that is the accreditation process, except that the accreditation process is for the organization and not for the people who lead the organization.

Bratton clearly articulates the basic issues of developing a professional police force and difficulty of developing committed police leadership for this country. Bratton has outlined the parameters of the problem, but, more important, some of the specific professional development needs that could be addressed by a more enlightened group of police leaders.

A College Degree and Its Value to a Police Officer

A question that often arises in conversations with police chiefs concerns the value of a college education for police recruits. After the riots in American cities in the late 1960s, the Kerner Commission and other oversight committees recommended that all members of the criminal justice profession have a college degree, particularly police officers.[1] The Law Enforcement Assistance Administration of the Department of Justice established the Law Enforcement Education Program, which provided stipends to attract new college graduates to the field of policing. Though financial support placed increased value on a college background, its impact was not universal. Many police leaders remained skeptical and were even threatened by the idea that a college-educated person might replace them. Others were concerned about their ability to provide the incentives for college graduates as they competed with businesses and other agencies for the best recruits. Finally, chiefs worried that college-educated recruits might generate demand for new directions and new methods of management, which would change a police culture already under stress. However, many chiefs acknowledged the benefits higher education would bring to the department and the community.

The Police Corps training program used a scenario-based training model, which introduced officers to the type of real-life situations they would face in their local communities. New recruits learned how to handle domestic violence calls, traffic stops, and other situations that required good judgment and the ability to talk with people. In addition, the Police Corps training offered experiences that reinforced a police department's commitment to community policing.

Charlie Sims, a former Hattiesburg, Mississippi, chief and the director of the Police Corps Staff Development School, has a unique perspective on police training and community policing, including the importance of training supervisors of line officers.

> In most states, I don't think the training is long enough or intensive enough. I don't think it focuses on making that officer well rounded and suited to deal with the complicated issues that are out there. I think that most states just concentrate on basic skills that are needed—such as driving, firearms, defensive tactics—and they don't spend time talking about leadership, community issues, and problem solving. It's just not important to them. Unfortunately, it's been that way for 25 years or more. They don't put enough into preparing officers effectively in their positions.
>
> If the line officer isn't going to get the training, then the department needs to invest in training for supervisors so that when they get a recruit fresh out of the academy, they can start developing them. The supervisors need to show them how to deal with the public and how to deal with the politics that come with the job and how to identify, analyze, and solve problems. They need to

teach them how not to go back to the same call, time and again, and realize that when their time is being wasted, they need to ask how can they change this and make a difference. If the supervisor is trained in all of those issues and can train their officers in the same way, then they will see some great results.

Chief Sims has identified a key area of professional development for line police officers. All of the chiefs acknowledge the importance of the role of the line supervisor in developing first-rate police officers. Unfortunately, there is limited training for police supervisors and many find themselves only transmitting their own first-line experience to their subordinates. Few supervisors are taught the value of giving feedback to their officers, let alone actually gaining top command support for providing this type of information to their staff.

Providence, Rhode Island, Chief Dean Esserman, who is also a lawyer, feels a college education would bring well rounded rather than narrowly trained people into the police department.

I've been overtaken by people in my life who were not college educated. What I don't like is that the college education draws the same people who are already attracted to this job, but now they go through the criminal justice education hoop where it's cops teaching new cops. That's not the role of education. I would like some of them to be poets. I would like them to study dance and drama and history and science, but not police science. I think that their career on the street is an education and if they value that they can also value the enlightenment that comes from a college education. The original point of requiring a college education was that an educated police officer would bring enlightenment, diversity, and understanding of complex problems to the profession. Unfortunately, with the rise of police science programs, it was just the same limited person with a new degree.

Some chiefs feel that a college education is best offered as an incentive to officers after they have entered the department. Given the continuing difficulty of recruiting and maintaining a high level of morale within the organization, they believe that requiring a college education could prevent people with good character but only a high school diploma from entering the profession. They suggest that a college education could serve as a valuable tool for developing an officer into a future leader.

Chief Ellen Hanson of Lenexa, Kansas, is very involved with succession planning and leadership development for many police departments across the country.

I have a strong opinion that it is not necessary for a new police officer to have a college degree. Some of my very best people don't. One in particular is at a stage where he's getting ready to retire and he would have been the next chief.

However, you won't be the police chief of Lenexa unless you have a BA degree and you should also be working on a master's degree. In our city culture, by the time you get to a chief's level, it is preferred that you have these degrees. It's not so important when you begin as an officer because I don't think it translates into making you a better cop. You're either going to be dedicated and outstanding in your career or you're not.

I have a brand new captain who went back to school because he knew that a college education would support his career development. He did a master's program in conflict resolution. Something like that where you're going to learn some constants is absolutely valuable. The reason I feel strongly about this is that it's become harder and harder to find good recruit candidates. It's more important to get a good candidate without a degree and encourage them and enable them to be excellent cops. I had a neighboring agency that for a while required a college degree and they made some bad hiring decisions in the process and passed up on some good cops.

You can always pick up a law book and learn the details. Officers have to know about things like probable cause or else they're going to make mistakes. They need to learn how to speak to people and help do public relations. Plus, in this day, technical language is vital. You're going to be behind the eight ball if you don't know that stuff. In my mind, it's more about understanding human relations than any book knowledge. You can front-load them with supervision at the beginning. I like the philosophy of asking how much you *can* do, rather how much you *can't* do. You encourage them to bring their own sense of style and not be so reticent. In my community, we watch real closely how people interact in the hiring process, which is not to say we don't make mistakes.

Most police chiefs would agree that it is necessary for supervisors and other senior command officers to have degrees, especially advanced training that provides valuable management and administrative skills. Still, the debate about the value of a college education for recruits remains central to the struggle to define police professionalism. Though recruiting of police officers has become a central issue in developing the police profession, it seems that giving up on the value of a college education is the wrong approach to dealing with the problem. More important, the police leadership needs to continue to maintain the value of education in order to provide the appropriate compensation for the important job of policing in our American communities. As our world becomes more complicated by a variety of political, social, and economic issues, it is critical that police officers have the technical education as well as the broad background that a college education can provide to make certain they are relevant and competent to address the many challenges that police officers face daily. A strategy of reducing the entry-level criteria for police officers seems counterproductive. One must reflect on Chief Bratton's earlier comments about the inability of the police profession to provide the necessary continuing education to ensure ongoing competence as well as future leadership.

Promoting an Officer's Ability to Communicate with People

The ability to relate to individuals and communities is a primary component of the community policing approach. Former Oakland California Police Chief George Hart tells a wonderful story about three New York police officers who came to Oakland for a 6-month leadership internship. At the conclusion of their stay, Hart invited them to dinner at his home and asked them about their observations of the Oakland police department. They told Hart that they really enjoyed the visit and the opportunity to meet so many fine police officers. However, they politely stated that they did not like how the department operated. They suggested that the officers "stand back from the people and they're aloof from the people. You don't relate to people. It's yes, ma'am; no, ma'am; just the facts, ma'am, that Jack Webb stuff." Hart admits that his own training experience as a "pup police officer" in the 1950s reinforced the idea that "you stood back from people, for you were now professionals."

Following the discussion with the New York City officers, Hart talked with his commanders, who agreed that they were "too isolated and delivery oriented; too hung up on the mechanics of the job." The feedback from the New York officers established the direction of Hart's leadership during his many years with the department, including many new approaches to building community relationships that predated the advent of community policing. His willingness to allow researchers into his organization also enabled others in the policing field to learn from the Oakland experience. Hart was one of the few leaders who saw the value of bringing outsiders into his department, but more important was a chief willing to listen, reflect, and, as appropriate, make changes to both his vision and the culture of his department. The implications of his leadership discoveries enabled the discussion about community policing to evolve during his tenure and during the decades following his retirement.

One of the younger chiefs who had learned about the lessons that Chief Hart experienced was Chris Magnus, the Richmond, California, police chief. Magnus agrees that teaching police officers to talk with people is a huge priority.

> I can't disagree with the issue of being able to talk to people being a top priority. For training, I think that's huge. We have too many officers, particularly younger officers, that have no idea how to talk to people or how to handle conflict. We have fostered the notion, thanks to Caliber Press [a police training book and manual company] and the whole street survival stuff that's been taken to a ridiculous extreme, that safety problems can be solved by technology

or more police officers, which is just insane. I don't know why, in any environment, one must come to this conclusion. In all fairness, Richmond is probably
worse because it really is dangerous for single officers to approach drug deals
by themselves on the street. This is a tough place. Having said that, I'm still
frustrated by the idea that everything has to be done by herd or pack, from
traffic stops to just talking to people on the street.

Magnus is trying to build a community policing-oriented culture in his
department. He has established a geographic district structure to decentral-
ize supervision and focus his officers on building stronger relationships with
the community.

They don't understand that their safety is more likely to come from the community than anywhere else. So the importance of building relationships in
the community is going to have more impact on their safety than all of the
technology and back up in the world. That's a hard one. The television show
Adam-12 knew more about community policing than a lot of cops today.

The Oakland Police Department is under continuing scrutiny by court-
appointed monitors, a community oversight board, and the mayor of the city
as a result of a series of leadership failures and negative interaction with the
community. Chief Wayne Tucker has a mandate to rebuild relationships with
the external community and reestablish a credible leadership group within
his organization. He believes training and supervision are critical human
resources management issues for this institutional reform.

Probably the internal management issue that's most problematic for us is
something called the personnel management system. Over the 10-year period
preceding me, we fell woefully short of any management system that assisted
us in daily operations of the organization. This personnel management system
would essentially provide a computerized system that could record histories
of individual officers. Tracking the officers gives us an opportunity for early
intervention if an officer has a problem. It also provides a clear history of the
officer's work in the department. This system takes a lot of the subjectivity
and anecdotal information about an officer and develops a real institutional
memory. The obvious benefits are to track what we think of as key indicators
of good or bad performance (complaints, punitive actions, commendations,
rewards). What's not quite so obvious is the need to be able to measure breadth
and depth of experience. We want a person to have a full career. We have people that have spent 5 years in the patrol division and repeated it five times for
25 years of service. That seems to me not to be what we're trying to do here.

Though many police officers reject the notion of being a social worker,
chiefs encourage them to communicate verbally rather using coercive force
to resolve many issues. Chiefs want to develop police officer self-confidence

through training, but express concern about the reliance on coercive force as a main tool for ensuring compliance with authority. Tucker recognizes that the Oakland Department has had to reorient its thinking in terms of the use of coercive force.

> It's coercive power and in our case, we've had a long standing history in the OPD of being pretty ham-fisted in terms of how we apply force. We need to become more contemporary and meet the changing expectations about the use of force. There are lots of ways to subdue people that don't cooperate with you. Most people don't resist in order to hurt you [meaning the police officer]. They just don't want to comply with your orders. Blunt-force trauma is not as effective as things like surgically applied force and pain compliance. That's really the key for us, whether it's blunt force or pain compliance. Pain compliance methods enable the force to subdue the person without hurting them. Blunt force generally requires a use of force which is not controllable and may be dangerous.

Tucker reflected on how he was changing the norms in his department around the issue of use of coercive force, including his own active persuasion methods and his strategies for building consensus.

> First of all, you start with the idea that change is going to happen. Then you try to manage the change so that you get the greatest degree of acceptance. However, after 41 years in this business, I think that behavior is more important than acceptance. There will forever be a group of people who will use their verbal skills and hypocrisy to say this is a bad idea and come up with 100 valid reasons why not to comply with the rule. In the end it's about behavior, that is, changing the police officer's behavior. You need to build consensus. The Police Officers' Association is a key part of this acceptance and they need to be on the front end of this discussion. So far, they've been reasonably accepting.

Tucker is proud of the new performance management system he has built in the department as a central component of Internal Affairs and personnel management operations. Other chiefs have discussed the internal discipline and motivation issues within their departments. The work of Tucker represents a key area of concentration for most of the police chiefs in this country.

Sergeants and Their Importance to the Chiefs' Leadership Efforts

Rick Fuentes, superintendent of the New Jersey State Police, has been implementing a wide range of oversight and accountability internal structures designed to manage officer performance following a racial profiling scandal and a federal consent decree. He has now established a credible, respectful relationship with not only the minority community but with all communities throughout the state. His relationship with his local communities has improved and he continues to reshape the culture of his police organization.

> The challenge we faced was lack of oversight and accountability. These have been addressed to some extent in big cities through Compstat. The oversight would require that we have the necessary technological improvements and reforms in place to be able to look at our police activity electronically. Then our supervisors would be able to manage their people in a very hands-on fashion. Our goal is to create new ranks of supervisors, ensure that there's a person reviewing the videotapes and in-car cameras, as well as offering regular counseling to officers in need of specific support. There are now multiple layers of review. Each one of them becomes a check and balance for the level below that level. When we're involved in a critical case, whether it's a consent search, use of force, or canine deployment, all of those videotapes in the cars are examined by the squad sergeant, station commander, troop commander, MAPS coordinator (this is our database), MAPS unit, and federal monitors. There are now seven or eight layers of review to ensure that the trooper is doing what they should be doing. If that's not the case, they get counseled very quickly. In most cases, it's a training issue and then we train the entire division.

As it turned out, Fuentes saw the number of layers of review as a budget windfall, especially in terms of the use of technology to monitor his officers' performance. Many other departments operating under consent decrees were exploring a similar process. Fuentes described his supervisory process to ensure compliance with the policy to prevent racial profiling.

> In 1999, the organization needed a lot of oversight, which because of poor technology, could not be accomplished. The sergeant inside a room with no windows was trying to make a decision on whether he should call off the pursuit or whether the trooper had a reasonably articulate suspicion in requesting a motorist to consent to a search. The sergeant was operating blindfolded and it wasn't logical to hold him accountable because he didn't have the tools to make him accountable. So that's what we did with our databases. The early warning system gave the sergeant a gigantic toolbox with live videotapes of officers' stopping cars that he could navigate, and by doing that he could pretty much drill down on anything.

Fuentes acknowledged that the technology has limits, but it provides the supervisor with a documented resource that can trigger training and counseling as needed. It also provides the specific performance management system that theoretically ensures the officer's compliance with the organization's mission and values.

In attempting to change organizational norms, Fuentes focused on the sergeants, because 50% of his troopers had come into the organization following the events of 1999. The key to the cultural shift that rewards officers for their ability to talk with people is the new early warning system regarding officer performance. Fuentes linked the training function more closely with the Internal Affairs unit so that the results of the early warning system lead to training and counseling for the officer. Fuentes has received strong accolades from his department and from the community for his efforts in changing not only his department's culture, but, more important, reducing both the perception and the reality of any state police officer's racial profiling on the highways in New Jersey. Fuentes's reorientation of his department has led to a directive from the governor ending the federal oversight in favor of the state police monitoring its own officers' performance. Fuentes challenged the norms of his department and created a new leadership culture, which embraced community policing through a respectful balance of both community engagement and enforcement.

Although police chiefs are proud of their successes, they are not unwilling to admit their mistakes. Some realize they made poor selections of senior commanders. They may have relied on friendship and personal loyalty and, in some cases, overlooked serious issues of respect and integrity when developing new leadership in a police culture that had been stagnant and condescending. Commissioner Frank Straub of White Plains, New York, focused on his sergeants as the key leadership factor for departmental change.

> To me, the most fundamental position in the department is the sergeant. You have to have sergeants that have a sense of ownership of the organization and are willing to take charge of your employees. That means identifying good people, rewarding them, and working with them to make them stronger people and stronger police officers. It also means identifying the people that have issues and dealing with those issues. That doesn't mean you have to discipline or arrest them, but it does mean intervention. So it really means having the sergeants have a sense of ownership and understanding that they are responsible for the people that work under them.

Straub spent a great deal of time talking with the sergeants and introduced changes in the sergeant ranks to ensure their support for the overall vision of the organization. He set new standards for their involvement with the community and encouraged a close working collaboration with local business owners. He also placed a high priority on the officers' ability to talk with the community and treat all people with respect.

> Getting them to have ownership of the organization versus coming to work and existing for 8 hours and then going home is a challenge. Demonstrating that we would support their decisions was important. If they made a bad decision

then we were going to work out why it was a bad decision. You can change any organization if you're committed to change. You have to find the people who are interested in changing the organization and convince them that you're believable and trustworthy. Ultimately, they're the ones that change the organization, not you. Here it was about picking out the key people, moving them into the right positions, and then giving them the ability to go and do what they had to do.

Straub gave his officers access to experiences that allowed them to see policing and community practices in different settings. He had his officers participate in a variety of external training programs at universities and visit the Holocaust museum as well as other departments. He has also collaborated with the nonprofit group North American Family Institute to develop an innovative Police/Youth Training Initiative designed to reduce youth violence and train his officers to talk with at-risk youth. This type of training and exposure had never been offered in the White Plains Police Department before Straub's administration. The positive impact of this training on the community, crime reduction, and the overall department has been well documented in the media.

An important motivational factor for officers is recognizing and acknowledging their service contributions to the department and the community. Research on worker performance indicates that employee recognition is also critical to building support for the organization's mission. Joe McNamara, former chief of Kansas City, Missouri, and San Jose, California, emphasized the importance of the chief's contact with line officers in this story:

One thing I learned from Clarence Kelly [former FBI director and Kansas City Police chief] initially wasn't my style, but he used to go down to each recruit class and read the canon of ethics. So I did that and then gave examples such as why you shouldn't take a free lunch because you can't be objective if you had to come back to that establishment for another reason. That was important. I greeted every class. When I got to San Jose, it was really sad. We had no internal newspaper. The union newsletter was just incredibly racist. There was inflammatory rhetoric about Latinos and so on. So we did our own newsletter. Then there was no ceremony at all in the department. Their attitude was we're cops and we're not into that. We got a lot of letters praising officers, and the secretary would just generate a response for me to sign. At first, I thought we'd just put them in their personnel file, but then all of the cops who seemed to be so tough starting yelling about their letters! Then the city council was complaining that they never saw any good stuff about cops, so we began to have awards ceremonies in the city council chambers. The council loved it because they were now on television and the officers loved it because they got public recognition for their good work.

McNamara started the San Jose recognition program in the late 1970s. He was a proponent of progressive policing and built a department recognized for its community involvement and crime-prevention methods. His personal commitment to developing police leaders who promote community policing has been recognized by the police profession for many years.

Significance of Training and Its Impact on the Department

Training is essential for teaching skills and defining good police work. In addition, it directly involves police officers in learning the organization's vision and mission. Chiefs also understand the importance of providing supervision and guidance for their police officers. Unfortunately, the police culture has not readily accepted supervision as a process that provides both controls and positive motivation. Police chiefs get pressure from outside monitors who intervene in their departments to make sure that police officer behavior is monitored regularly and corrected when necessary. Many are establishing their own internal personnel management systems to identify officers who are resisting implementing the department's vision. Though police training is of critical importance to all police leaders, the reality is that most programs are still time bound with limited creativity.

Training programs such as the Police Corps used innovative, adult-learning methods to develop communication skills and established new approaches to the use of coercive force by police officers. The programs also had creative training strategies designed to introduce police recruits to community policing and direct engagement of the community. Although these training approaches have not been universally accepted, they have at least created new opportunities for a dialogue about police training and the role of police officers in the community. Recruiting problems in urban police departments underscore the challenge of insuring that the profession has a strong contingent of educated, dedicated officers who understand the value and dynamics of community policing. Recruiting challenges include issues of compensation, assignment, and skills development, which also raise fundamental questions about the importance and value of the police profession in American society. The private security sector is also having an impact as communities question the allocation of police resources and use of tax revenue. Police chiefs must give the public evidence of the value of their profession and demonstrate positive performance on a daily basis.

In addition to the daily challenges of policing, police chiefs must also think about succession and future police leadership. Though they all acknowledge the importance of the role of first-line supervisors in implementing their vision, few departments have developed leadership-training plans. Sergeants and lieutenants are the principal leaders of the line officers,

but few receive training and feedback to help them carry out their development and supervisory responsibilities. Many chiefs have begun to explore
new strategies for the development of police leaders, but little has been done
to build on the strong recruit-training efforts of programs such as Police
Corps. This chapter about developing a good police officer highlights key
training components that should be included in the formulation of a future
police leadership program.

Internal Politics, the Police Chief, and Police Officer Empowerment

7

At a University of California conference on police empowerment in the fall of 2006, participants focused on how to empower and engage police officers in a process of shared leadership and community policing. One of the conference speakers, Wesley G. Skogan, offered the following comments in a conference paper:

> It is necessary to be clear-eyed about the difficulties of innovating in police organizations. Because of widespread enthusiasm for innovations such as community policing among academics and the informed public, it could appear that reform comes easily. In fact, it is hard, the political risks involved are considerable, and efforts to change the police often fall far short or fail. Discussions of policing reform also often feature modern management terms such as *employee empowerment*. This also makes senior managers very nervous. They worry about laziness, corruption, racial profiling, and excessive force, and they do not trust rank-and-file officers on any of those.[1]

Skogan essentially encouraged police leaders to directly involve their line police officers in all aspects of policing but cautions police chiefs to recognize the obstacles. When promoting the concept of support for community policing, police leaders must actively engage the line officers and the police union in the implementation of this strategy. After a review of data at a Compstat meeting in Baltimore, where there was a very committed police leadership team, the deputy commissioner, Marcus Brown, noted:

> We seem to get it about problem solving and crime prevention, but the fact is that only those of us in the room really understand what is happening. We need to get this message down to the troops so they know what we're trying to do.

The deputy commissioner's comment underscores the lack of connection between the department's leadership vision and the rank-and-file officers. The new generation of young officers, who may not be prepared or willing to just accept orders, wants to know why they are doing a specific set of tasks.

Any discussion about strategies for morale building, retention, and professional development has to recognize the strengths and limitations of the police culture and the internal politics of the entire organization. The Police Corps's innovative training incorporated the issue of internal politics into its entire training program. There were active discussions about what a new officer would do when confronted by the norms of the existing police culture. One young officer told a story about how he was gung ho coming out of the training academy and really wanted to work hard on his midnight shift assignment. He was confronted by an experienced officer who told him that he should slow down as the older officer "liked to take a nap from 2 to 3 in the morning." The young energetic officer had to calm down and not be so aggressive about patrolling the community all night. In addition, he had to recognize some realities about the police work ethic, culture, and internal politics. This chapter explores the internal politics of a department and its impact on the police chief's vision, as well as the individual and organized elements of the police culture that police chiefs interact with on a daily basis.

Chiefs' Experience with Police Unions

Police unions grew out of the economic and political turmoil that confronted police agencies in the 1970s. Many departments faced serious budget challenges, and communities were suspicious of the police management's ability to control officers. Police unions were formed to provide political representation and ensure appropriate financial compensation and support when officers got into trouble with their superiors. Chief Darrel Stephens, of the Charlotte–Mecklenburg (North Carolina) Police Department, has interacted with unions for a number of years in a number of locations, with both negative and positive reactions about his experience with police unions.

> I've had a variety of different experiences with unions. The worst was in St. Petersburg, Florida, and two of the best were in Key Largo [Florida] and in Lawrence, Kansas. I don't have a problem with unions advocating for officers' benefits and salaries. I don't have a problem with them defending officers in different disciplinary kinds of issues. The experience in St. Petersburg was that union leaders basically envisioned their role as staying in office. For the union to stay in office, they create an us-against-them atmosphere within the department. That's pretty counterproductive. They don't care about the community. They care about being in office and being able to say that they protected specific individual officers.
>
> I was hired in St. Petersburg in the midst of a no-confidence vote on the chief, and a lot of problems were evident. When I came in, they were fairly unreasonable people, but fortunately, we were able to work through the issues. My first 2 days, I was assistant chief and there was "work speed up," which had officers doing their work but rapidly and not very carefully. They had been trying to negotiate an agreement with the city for 5 or 6 months and it didn't happen. They had set the date for the union action. We were able to work through those issues. Pay and benefits were part of it, but what the department needed more was structure and training.

Stephens has a national reputation for working productively with his officers and the unions, as evidenced by the strong relationship that he has built in the Charlotte–Mecklenburg department. There is now a recognition that officers offer a great deal to their departments and the community using the problem-solving model of policing. Unfortunately, unions still primarily focus on personnel complaints, benefits, and compensation. However, the Police Corps was able to mobilize support from police unions when it recognized the value of police training to support officer safety and potentially develop a new mandate for the line police officer.

David Couper served for about 20 years in Madison, Wisconsin, from the 1970s to the 1990s. He worked closely with University of Wisconsin law professor Herman Goldstein developing the problem-solving model of policing. Couper was a visionary who saw a constructive role for the police in the community. He was a strong advocate of enabling his police officers to solve problems as they arose rather than just respond to calls for service. Still, he faced many serious challenges from unions as he tried to develop this new approach to policing. Couper describes his interaction with the unions.

> I changed my initial views about police unions. The union was a detriment and an impediment for the first 10 years of my work in Madison. I was pretty much combating with them and going to arbitration and those kinds of things. We looked at the number of hours that we spent in arbitration and I finally got to the point of saying, "How do we work together?" We all really want the same things. Maybe in those first years I needed a union to protect myself from myself because the chief has a lot of power and they feel very vulnerable. The change occurred when we considered the union to be a player and join the management team. People said they would challenge us when it came to promotions and I said absolutely, but they are going to be held to the same level of confidentiality that the command staff is. That is, what you hear and say here, stays here. Well, they asked, if they did abide by it, did it mean they could come in, and I said absolutely. But they didn't want to get themselves compromised, so what they did was go and get a cup of coffee when our team agenda was presented. This agenda usually included some sensitive personnel issues which could have compromised the union's role in representing the officers. When the discussion was over they would come back in again. But there was a level of trust that wasn't there before we made these changes.

Couper was a chief during a tumultuous political period in the 1970s. With all the student demonstrations, he had to ensure that his own rank and file followed the law and worked with the community. When asked what changed his mind about the unions, Couper told the following story:

> A large group of officers signed a petition against me and there were all kinds of hearings. It was pretty vicious. Some officers went to the hearings and

perjured themselves and I took notes like a good investigator. I said that if they screwed with me, then there would be a day of reckoning. So the hearings ended, and I had some really good, civilian management lawyers on my defense team and they did some creative work to resolve the conflict in our favor. People were happy that I won the case. I then turned to my staff of lawyers and asked what we should do now. He said his recommendation was to forget about all of it and move on, even though it hurt deeply. I thought about it for a day and decided to not engage in any more pettiness with the union. It was the best advice that I had ever gotten. I listened to the advice of the lawyers for good reasons and we moved forward in a positive atmosphere with the union.

Couper made a conscious decision to stop being an adversary of his own staff and the union, and move toward a problem-solving model of leadership. Couper recognized that the role of police officers was fundamentally to solve problems in the community. With this in mind, he reoriented his leadership style and embraced officers who were creative about solving local community problems. His strategy elevated the officers to a more professional role and enabled him to withdraw from the petty bickering that had been a norm in the department. This enabled him to continue to build his vision and serve successfully as the Madison police chief. He left policing after more than 25 years and now serves as a minister in a local community near Madison.

There was a provocative incident in one of Heather Fong's districts in San Francisco, which involved disturbing charges of public insensitivity and racism. When addressing the behavior of her officers and the district command leadership, she realized that she had to confront all of the negative internal norms that undermined a more constructive, community-oriented leadership for her department. She describes her approach to establishing a new set of criteria for promotion.

It's an interesting time because you always hear that morale is down. Why is it down? I think it's down because the officers are used to doing things a certain way. No accountability. I have a relationship with the union, but it's not a relationship that I feel is supportive at this time. In the past, it's always been you do this for me and I'll do this for you. But I've told people not to lobby me about promotions. I will follow the criteria as outlined by civil service rules and select the most qualified candidates for the job. I wanted to take the internal politics and a lot of the nepotism and patronage out of the job-selection process. You want to talk about disciplinary cases, let's talk about reasonable and realistic dispositions. I think because of my approach, they don't know what to expect. I won't go to them and say, "I'm going to make X number of appointments." I just promoted 7 captains. You can imagine the letters and phone calls. I do not talk to people about promotions. So don't even try. These are the things that people are not clear about because it's a different way of doing things.

When Fong tried to make changes in the appointment process for her deputy chiefs, she ran into obstacles created by the police culture and lack of clarity in the overall mission for the department. She also met resistance from the city's strong municipal unions and the rigid civil service system.

Deputy chiefs and commanders are exempt positions, meaning I can make the appointments. It's not the good old boys [I promote], it's the people who are committed to their jobs, who are professional, and will make tough decisions and not necessarily popular decisions. Gee, my life would be easy if everything was a popular decision. You can't do that. That's the culture that people have been used to for too long. For a while it was the friends of whomever the chief was that got promoted. That's wrong. I'm going to focus on talent and my belief that the person can do a good job.

Even when she has been promoting the overall needs of the department with other political bodies, Fong has felt frustrated.

I do not believe that this union supports me. They've not come out and said that to me but I think part of it is that they want things to be status quo. I'm not that person. If they truly cared about the membership, we would work hand and hand, but they're not there.

Chief Fong had to build a strong relationship with the mayor to ensure support for her tenure. She continues to feel strongly about doing the right thing and changing the culture of the department for greater respect from the community. She has focused carefully on rebuilding a police culture that mirrors the needs of the community while supporting the positive values of police professionalism. In addition, she has renewed her efforts to rebuild a more constructive relationship with the union. She recognized the difficulties of the past relationship, which generated some serious community relations issues. Though the San Francisco Police Department has been embroiled in some difficult challenges internally within the past few years, Fong has mobilized the support of the mayor and created some new opportunities for constructive dialogue with the unions and the community.

Strategies for Working with the Union

Many chiefs have established close working partnerships with their unions, as they are a powerful political voice that can assist with police recruitment

and retention efforts. Former Police Chief Lee Brown recalls his experience
with unions.

> They differ and they changed over the years. New York was a very sophisti-
> cated police union. They have their annual banquet and every politician in
> the state is there. I came to Houston when two unions were competing for
> members. Neither was supportive of me for a number of reasons. First of all
> because I was from the outside, not even from Texas, and I was an African
> American and that created a lot of difficulties with the unions. The major
> police union now is the Houston Police Officers Association. It has changed
> tremendously and is very sophisticated. They give money to politicians. They
> go to Austin and lobby. They learned from the New York PBA [Patrolmen's
> Benevolent Association] that you now have to be sophisticated and political
> to get what you want.

Brown had a number of strategies for getting what he wanted from
the unions.

> You have to work with them. They have a responsibility to their membership.
> The best way to work with unions is to get them involved with what you're
> doing. They are not unreasonable people. I had the union come to my com-
> mand staff meetings. They had a voice. We worked with a lot of other organi-
> zations as well. The key is to listen, first of all, and then do what you say you're
> going to do. Each time I had a meeting with the union, I would send a letter
> back to them saying this is what we discussed and what I've done about it.
> Police chiefs should not be afraid of a union; that's the bottom line. I'll give
> you an example. When I was here, I wanted to change the decal on the police
> cars. That's not a big deal, but it's also part of the tradition of this depart-
> ment. I brought the union in and talked about it and told them that I wanted
> it changed but we'd keep a smaller version of our badge on the car as well to
> maintain the tradition. Well, they went out and put it in their paper before we
> made the change. There were no surprises and they supported me. If I had just
> gone ahead and done it without telling them, you can bet that they would be
> opposing it.

When Brown arrived in Houston, he did not replace the top commanders
but instead persuaded his entire department to follow his vision and implement a variety of changes, including a focus on community policing. His
leadership style involved a clear recognition of the value of line police officers
and their problem-solving potential, along with the critical importance of
the union's involvement with change. This approach has brought him accolades from line officers, researchers, and ultimately members of the many
communities in which he served.

Chris Magnus, the Richmond, California, chief, has been president of a
police union as well as a police chief. Based on this unique perspective, he

appreciates that history and context must be part of establishing a working relationship with the union.

> I've had it both ways. I was a union president in Lansing, Michigan, and I've worked my way up as a cop. My master's degree is in labor relations, so it's an area that I'm interested in. In Fargo, North Dakota, I had no union, whereas here I have several unions. It's a lot like my experience with civilian review boards. I meet regularly with the unions.
>
> They were really burned by what happened when Richmond went through some tough financial times. They really felt they got screwed and were very embittered. There's no trust between the unions and the administration of the city, even though it's a new city leadership team. It's their history. They are still suspicious and angry, and don't care whether I'm new or not. They try to find things to be angry about, but I really haven't had much problem with the union so far.

Mobilizing officers to support a new community policing-oriented direction started with establishing new geographic districts in Richmond. This was an entirely new concept as prior chiefs had centralized all police authority and accountability. Magnus then initiated a Compstat accountability system to track the performance of his officers. Another tough decision was promoting a lieutenant to deputy chief, a major challenge to the former system, which only rewarded seniority not officer performance. The union and the police officers resisted many of his changes and Magnus was well aware of the potential for negative reaction to future changes.

> I think the reaction will be huge to this effort. You don't put something like this in place in 6 months. We haven't even scratched the surface. They are okay with it right now. I know when things aren't going well because I'll ask cops, "What's your impression of the situation and how things are going?" If they say, "Well, the truth of the matter is that I go out and do my job like I always have," then I know that I must be doing a rotten job as the chief. I would much rather hear that the officers are pissed off about the changes! Right now, they seem to think I'm pretty approachable and these seem like good ideas. Yeah, it's a little extra work and stuff but that's not all bad. We're getting more equipment and more training, and we just settled a contract that's pretty good.

Despite potential resistance to change and the continuing challenges of violence reduction in his community, Magnus sees himself as part of a new generation of police leadership: "I am a change agent. I advertise myself this way; at least they know what they're getting. If they don't like that then all I can say is that I'm not the status quo."

Magnus is now part of a new city administration committed to reducing violence and building a safer community. He is the principal architect of the community-oriented policing model and is working diligently to mobilize support from both the community and his officers. A new police union contract has given him some latitude to move forward with his union on issues of compensation and benefits. Though he has made some significant progress, discussions continue about shifts toward district-oriented, problem-solving policing strategies.

Chiefs Confront Officer Empowerment Challenges

Former Chief George Hart of the Oakland police department was a key facilitator of the internal support that enabled his boss, Charles Gain, and researcher Hans Toch to develop a peer-review process for officers. This involved creating a new process for reviewing police behavior issues. In addition, this process supported developing new methods and practices to reduce police officer misuse of coercive force. This unique peer-review process directly conflicted with the hierarchal system of control and command in which only the officers' direct supervisor addressed any issues of problematic police behavior. In many cases, supervisors avoided conflicts with their subordinates and generally avoided any situation that would require giving real feedback to their subordinates. Toch's book, *Agents of Change: A Study of Police Reform*, documents the power and scope of this first effort to empower police officers to give feedback and support to their fellow officers within the police culture.[2] Hart also assisted with the transformation of the Oakland police officers' association into a union in the mid-1970s.

Chief Hart described himself as a "police professional manager" during the era of strong, hierarchal police organizations. Though he subscribed to a military model, he had a reputation among his officers as an approachable, engaging police chief. He recalls the emerging police unions and their reach into the organization, as well as internal politics and the relationship between a chief and the unions.

An association is more of a professional body of interest or a body for a specific purpose, not just for benefits and wages, but it has a broader association and commonality. To an extent, this may be a totally fictitious definition, but a union was in their mind. Old timers in the associations make a strong case that we're not a union, but we are an association. In the Oakland situation, they had binding arbitration for years. If you didn't agree with the decision, you could go to an arbitrator for resolution. There were some cases, in spite of a good relationship, that became more difficult to handle. The leadership of the organization began to get more strident, more demanding, and more political. They were getting cozy with politicians and seeing who they could back and support for office. We were saying that there was no prohibition against that as an association or a union, but it was not appropriate for an individual. This was not what officers should be investing in professionally. The chief's job is above all else to serve as a moat between the external world and the internal world of the organization so that the internal world can do its job. Chiefs absolutely need to be the focal point for addressing external influence. They need to shield everything below that, professionally at least, not from input but from interference.

This was Hart's experience with unions as they established themselves within the police department and as part of the larger political environment. Although their primary focus was economic, unions became more actively involved in operational issues, including deploying police resources. Hart found this level of involvement by the unions to be intolerable and he confronted the union directly about its assault on his territory. His message was, "I will not talk about deployment and we will not negotiate because I will not let somebody else decide how we're going to operate this department." The union allowed him to play out his myth.

> The department and the union had a mutual agreement that we would not discuss those issues because they knew that I wouldn't tolerate it. They also knew that they could force it if they wanted to. They could've said we don't care if you want to talk or not, here's what you're going to do that's the end of it, but they never did that. Once an agreement was reached that limited the union's role to negotiations over salaries and benefits, the relationship was fine. In addition, we worked out a policy that allowed us to handle individual officers' discipline cases and again, these discussions with the union were always professional, open, and fair.

Though Hart developed a good working relationship with the union, he did negotiate one agreement about deployment of resources that he describes as "the worst decision that I made with a union."

> We had a lot of deployment issues and discussion about 10-hour shifts and other strategies. We were looking for a strategy that would be of interest to the troops because we were having a lot of retention problems and losing people big time. We knew that the shift schedule might offer a way of dealing with the problem, so we looked at a lot of alternative plans for about a year and finally came up with a model I felt comfortable with. Part of this new plan put us on permanent shifts, whereas up until that time we had various shift times and rotated shifts. We all shook hands on this new plan, although I said it was an experiment. I was worried about certain features of the permanent shifts and what it might do to the culture of the organization. If we saw any negative changes, such as absenteeism, accidents, or other adverse change in productivity, we'd go back to the other shift arrangements.

I quickly came to realize the new plan wasn't working. It impacted the department culture and we were beginning to become three different departments. I decided that we should go on for another 6 months and then go back to the other shift rotations. The union president refused to agree to stop the permanent shifts. He told me that the troops loved the agreement for permanent shifts and couldn't go back to the old arrangement. I said this was a breach of the agreement. He said, "Yes, we know." It was not good that it happened and was very hurtful to our relationship. We continued on, but it was very different.

Despite his comments about unions being more strident, Hart felt he had generally managed a good working relationship with the union. Still, it is evident that Hart was disappointed by confronting his union and clearly not satisfied with the outcome of their negotiations. Hart was considered a strong manager of his department, and was well respected by both management and line officers. The bargaining process with the union was part of a newly emerging management and union partnership of the 1970s. Hart was ambivalent about its value, and the negotiation with the union around deployment of officers remains a discomforting episode in his memories of his tenure as chief of police in Oakland. Clearly, Hart's own description of himself as the professional manager left little room for real empowerment of his officers, let alone a union telling him how to deploy his police officer resources.

In spite of Hart's discomforting tales about his union relationship, a police chief needs to build a collaboration that works for both the department and the officers. Former Tulsa Police Chief Drew Diamond had grown up in his department so he was familiar with unions and the internal politics of his organization.

Police chiefs have to understand a couple of things. Unions are about the membership. Sometimes it's only about union leadership. Sometimes the unions are divided along racial lines, so we see the Black officers association or coalitions of Hispanic officers. In some cases, the police unions have failed to represent the interests of their minority members. So in one sense, the mission of the unions is only about themselves. There's virtually nothing in their charters about police service and the rest of the community. There's nothing in the contracts that requires a certain style, a certain vision of policing, milestones for protecting the communities. It's all about showing up for work and getting paid. Here are the benefits and here are the grievance rules. Police chiefs have to recognize that unions are not about service, in terms of basic policing.

Despite these rather provocative comments, Diamond still encourages chiefs to actively involve the unions in all problem-solving approaches to working with the community. He supports ensuring that officers are at the table when the tough financial, deployment, or other resource allocation issues must be solved, and he believes the relationship between the chief and the union is pivotal.

> When the relationship between the union and police department is in disarray, the police service is in disarray. At best, you're getting mediocre service, and at worst, you're getting really bad service because what's on everyone's mind is how they're being treated as opposed to how they're serving the community.

Diamond was a respected trainer for the Police Corps. He found police unions strongly supportive of the program once they determined that the training approach was a potential avenue for salary increases, as well as an innovative strategy to enhance the police profession. However, as a police chief, Diamond confronted serious challenges from unions when he tried to open his department to a more diverse group of police officer candidates. His advice about negotiating with unions is based on both successes and failures.

> I would advise you to put the unions at the table, always be transparent and candid, and remove your ego from the discussion. I didn't learn this until it was too late. You've got to remove yourself from the idea that the union is out to get you and the world is coming to an end. You've got to stick with the vision and mission and do your best to get them involved with your direction through building a relationship with them.

Former Commissioner Leonard Hamm of Baltimore, Maryland, worked closely with the unions throughout his career and has a good reputation for working with line officers as well as commanders.

> I've been very successful with the union only because they are so disorganized that they don't have time to worry about me. The union leadership is doing a bunch of foolish stuff that's not impacting the department. It's not embarrassing the department, but it's rendering them ineffective. My attitude is that we all work for the betterment of the people who work in this agency. Let's sit down and talk. It's not about me being in charge. I never come with that attitude. It's about how we can do right by our people within the rules and with the money we have.
>
> You've got to pay attention to the individuals running the unions. Unions can be weak and dependent on the individual leader. They can also be strong and dependent on the same leader. As a chief, you have to be able to change your personality in order to deal with that individual leader because there are some personalities running unions that will try to take over the agency. You've got to make sure that this doesn't happen. In my case, I created a vision for the department that resonated with the union because basically we're all cops. I told the union that whatever decision they make must represent all the cops. They understood that and so far we're on the right track together.

Hamm faced serious external challenges from the state's attorney in Baltimore over an early policy of zero tolerance with street crime. Hamm was able to mobilize strong union support until he was caught in the middle of a bitter mayoral election, and negotiations between the city of Baltimore and its police union. Unfortunately, the escalating murder rate and political support for strict law enforcement overshadowed his best efforts to develop a community policing model for the city. Nevertheless, he was well respected for his ability to communicate with his officers as well as the community. He advises developing a clear understanding with the unions about their role in the department. He further stresses the value of engaging all officers in supporting enforcement of the law while enlisting the assistance of people in the community.

Morale, Empowerment, and Officer Performance

Jane Perlov, former chief of Raleigh, North Carolina, and a longtime New York City Police Department commander, thinks that morale and empowering police officers are key issues. She was an outsider when she came to Raleigh, but spent more than 5 years there. Her reputation for building positive morale was well known throughout the department. She offered these ideas about how she approached this important organizational issue.

> I measure the morale in different ways. Of course, there are always different people that talk to you about things. They're kind of appointed to do that. So I utilize them often. I'm out and about a lot and I talk with officers about what's going on. I'll call the union guys in for a talk. It's interesting because this is a right-to-work state. There are two different unions that work down here, a Police Benevolent Society and a police union association, but they are really informal associations because there's no collective bargaining in this right-to-work state. Still I utilize them and I talk to them on a steady basis. Before I make a police change I talk with them. I also involve cops in all our focus groups, including the internal communications group, external communications group, vacation group, and the tactics group. We just rewrote all of our departmental operational orders, which had never been rewritten before. I rewrote them positively by saying "this is what you should do" rather than "what you shouldn't do." We put the values with each procedure, values that we agreed on as a department. I think it was unusual for a department to involve and empower officers in this way.
>
> The involvement of the officers has been pretty extensive but it's made a huge difference. Actually the union used to come in here with a big list. Now their biggest complaint is that there's no soap in the men's room. I still make the decisions, but I ask the officers all the time.

Perlov's experience as an empowering, engaging police leader offered a new style for police leadership in her city, but also earned praise from her state's police executive leadership ranks. Her engaging management style embraces the theme of empowerment or as some chiefs say, "How do I get my officers to buy in to community policing approaches that I think will work for them?"

In a February 2007 gathering of 25 chiefs from midsized cities convened in White Plains, New York, by the Department of Justice's COPS office, there was consensus that the majority of police officers still do not understand the community policing model, let alone feel empowered and engaged in problem-solving approaches. Nor did attendees feel many chiefs had the ability to promote support for this reform, even within a top-down paramilitary hierarchy.

Robert Olson has also had extensive experience working with police unions and internal politics in Yonkers, New York, and Minneapolis, Minnesota. He's a strong supporter of engaging officers in community policing approaches as he understands the empowerment it creates for line police officers.

> Police unions were one of the best things that ever happened in law enforcement in the context of getting wages and respect for officers. Their mantra was a clean uniform and polished shoes. They accomplished all of this in the 1970s. Then there was a tipping point, when the issues of working conditions, benefits, and wages were saturated. The power of the unions was waning a little bit so they dipped into management, which they should have never been allowed to do. Unions now foster mediocrity. That's where the rub with management now is. I even tried to have them tell me who the best cops were and they won't go there because they would have to say, "Joe, they didn't give you that raise because you're no good."

Unions might have had a role in promoting the police officer performance management or early warning systems used to identify officers who are potential behavioral risks. However, it seems that their support has been negligible and that they focus primarily on specific issues involving individual officers. Olson has his own take on the productivity of police officers and police unions.

> We've created hoops that they have to jump through and everybody knows that if they jump through this one, they get an A, and if they jump through this one, and then they get a B. That's okay with them because then they're not accountable and it's not about who's better than whom. It's the whole seniority thing in police hierarchies. I've got seniority and this degree and this is what the promotion is all about for officers. When you talk about a system where their commanders can rate one Joe as an 8 and someone else as a 5, that's a no, no. It's too subjective because they can't handle the howling they're going

to get from the guys at the bottom who were rated poorly. They won't go there and that's the biggest problem.

With my union, I could only appoint five inspectors and three deputy chiefs because the union was more powerful in the state legislature and got a specific state law passed that said that the police chief can't do more than appoint to these positions. That's where the unions have gone in the past years. They're now pushing for an officers' bill of rights, which would stop police chiefs from evaluating performance and giving merit increases. They come to their associations and say over the next 3 years, we propose a 12% pay increase. The union has to come back and tell the government what they're going to do to earn the raise. Now the reality is that they don't do squat differently and they still get the raise. But what a concept!

Although he has been in many challenging circumstances that have been threatening both professionally and personally, Olson's commitment to community policing remains strong. This was evident when he provided the project direction for a Police Executive Research Forum (PERF)-sponsored program in Jamaica, which directly confronted police corruption and high levels of violence and fear in the local communities. The new community policing framework reduced violence and engaged both the police and the community in a constructive set of collaborative activities that supported the basic vision of community policing and problem solving. Olson and his colleagues mobilized the entire community to rebuild local bridges, establish job programs, reenergize local education programs, and specifically target local criminals who were disrupting life in the community. The success of this program has been well documented by PERF and the U.S. Department of Justice.

Olson has lectured extensively about the police culture, organizational transformation, and the tenure of chiefs. His most difficult challenge as a police chief came when he confronted the police and political culture of the Yonkers, New York, police department. He offers this reflection on how to meet such a challenge.

If you're able to throw your ego away and are consistently willing to compromise and be reasonable and bend in what you do and yet not give up your integrity, but possibly some of your pride, you'll survive longer. However, you have to go into this business with the idea that they're going to get rid of you at some point. If you're consistently doing the right thing and weaving through issues without hurting your integrity you'll last longer. Eventually if you're doing the right thing as a leader, you're going to confront many "sacred cows" of the department. Some departments try to change their culture, while others do their best to preserve their "cows." That's why even the good chiefs last only 3 to 3½ years. It catches up to them and the politics just kills them.

Olson's observations about managing and evaluating officer performance provide a framework for exploring the merits of the Compstat accountability system. There is limited evidence that Compstat has been able to focus on an individual officer's performance. The internal culture has yet to embrace strategies that link officer performance to specific outcomes on the street. Many unions have strongly resisted any type of officer performance differentiation systems or use of merit pay. Chiefs are still trying to create an early warning system that identifies problems with officers' behavior. In addition, new forms of officer recognition and acknowledgment for community policing and problem-solving methods have not yet been formally developed, let alone implemented.

Compensation and benefits remain central issues for all police officers. Of equal importance, many committed officers are looking to assume leadership posts within the department. Departments commonly rely on a seniority system to establish the framework for promotions. Many departments link promotion to a civil service system that uses longevity as a criterion for the opportunity to apply for a promotion within the department. Promotions of police officers have been a central leadership issue during Bill Landsowne's tenure as a police chief in San Diego, California.

> The promotional process is a difficult challenge. Everybody thinks they're the best; they really do. Everybody wants to get promoted. You go out and promote somebody, and you get into this confrontation about how did you do it, I'm better than they are, what criteria did you use. They want a matrix as opposed to looking at the work history. I'll look at 10 people and pick the one that I think is best. I'm right on the money most of the time. Every once in a while I make a mistake, but that comes with the territory. But the unions want to know why you did it. I've negotiated in three different cities on how to do a promotional process. You do the internal and external interviews, how the scoring goes, and review the types of questions you've asked, and then once you get all of that together, you look at their performance and grade it.

Although it would seem obvious to make work history and performance part of the promotion process, the unions' focus on seniority collides dramatically with performance-based indicators of a police officer's service in the community. Few police organizations have feedback mechanisms that support candid, fair assessments of officers' performance. Unfortunately, the police culture has been reluctant to provide consistent feedback methods for officers, preferring to wait until there is a problem that must be addressed. Again, the discussions about the relevance of leadership education and a supervisory force that is both willing and capable of providing candid feedback for line officers have crippled many departments' efforts to promote a career path for police officers based on merit and job performance.

Chiefs' Final Thoughts on Police Unions
and Officer Empowerment

Lansdowne has his own perspective on police chiefs' relations with police unions.

> I've been with three unions and they've been exactly the same. They want professionals working for them. They want good working conditions, good compensation, good equipment, and good training. But when push comes to shove, the union leadership's first responsibility is to the members, then the police department, and then the city. That's their priority line. My role [as a police chief] is just the opposite. My priorities are to the city, to the department, and then the individual officer. So as we begin to make decisions, we both want the same things but we make decisions in a different fashion. If push comes to shove, I'm going to do what's best for the city and they're going to go with what's best for that labor contract. I'm saying to them that we have a real financial problem in the city of San Diego. We don't have the money to pay you this year. We'll get there, but we don't have it now. Their position is that we don't care about them; we should stand in front of the train and get killed because they want the money.

Gil Kerlikowske, the Seattle police chief, found that union relations vary greatly in different geographic areas.

> I had a vote of no confidence a little over a year ago. I actually had two in my career as chief. It's an interesting thing. The Northwest unions are a little different. They can be a little more difficult to deal with than other unions. In Buffalo [New York], they're very powerful, well funded, strategic, organized, and it's a tough environment. It was great for me with them because they were a union focused on overtime, seniority, salary, and benefits. They didn't really have an interest in running the department. They had been kicked around a lot, their salaries were low, and their equipment was not very good. There was a huge amount of political attention on any promotion and transfer. So it actually worked out incredibly well for me.
>
> I came to Seattle and guess what? Salary, benefits, equipment, training, facilities are really very good. The union wasn't full time even though it was a big union of 1,100 members. But they could be very prickly over little things. The thing that pushed them over the edge with the vote of no confidence was an officer who got a written reprimand. They couldn't believe this was being done to him. The union asked me to take the discipline back because Chief Sanders had delegated discipline to an assistant chief, so I took it back. Be careful what you wish for. I'm on my fourth union president in 6 years, so that's been a little difficult.

Kerlikowske recognizes the fine line a chief must walk when dealing with unions. He had recently been a guest speaker at a meeting of the top

50 police unions (a first invitation ever for a chief), where he focused on the importance of treating officers and the union with respect in spite of differences.

> I think understanding and recognizing the unions' importance and how you deal with them is very important to the department. You don't want to be at war with them over every issue and you also want them to know where the line in the sand is on different things, too.

Nevertheless, Kerlikowske is not enthusiastic about participatory management strategies designed to empower and engage line officers in the operational activities of the department. This model of participation can be used to enhance the power of the police unions or, in some cases, undermine the legitimate collective bargaining role of the unions when they engage in discussions of salaries, work rules, or discipline.

> I've looked at participatory management [which is designed to "involve" line officers in the department's activities] and I know a lot of purists say that you don't have it unless the line officers are really involved. I remember Neil Behan [retired Baltimore County chief and an early developer of the police problem-solving models] telling me one time that he made a really good decision on a community policing project because the officer involved called the county executive personally and said he felt they really needed to have a particular tree cut down. The county executive called Neil and said, "What the hell is this officer calling me for?" Neil said, "I know that it's working when they feel empowered to do that."
>
> I'm more like [William] Bratton on this empowerment issue. We hire a lot of new people who don't always have a lot of police experience, and we're giving them a pretty wide parameter for the decisions they can make on the street. I want upper-level commanders to be the directors and problem solvers. It should all be from on high, but it should be driven from the lowest level because they don't always have the kind of background knowledge and experience to be making some pretty important decision on some pretty complex stuff. I would think that the precinct captains, lieutenants, and sergeants are a better way to go with the actual problem-solving decisions.

William Bratton was clear about why he was introducing the Compstat model in New York City. In his mind, the system depended on the police commanders' ability to follow through on issues raised in each accountability review session and be held accountable for the resolution of any identified problem. Some chiefs recognize the need for accountability systems that involve line officers more directly, but approaches to empower them remain in a state of development.

Significance of Internal Politics and Police Leadership

The internal politics of a police organization are complicated by its culture and norms. Penetrating the culture to mobilize support for a new vision or mission can be challenging. Mobilization of union support is not an easy task but definitely a necessary one. All of the chiefs interviewed acknowledged the challenges of the internal departmental politics and many have successfully courted union involvement in implementing their vision. Others chiefs have had difficulties in getting police unions to broaden their views and support the development of community policing. They acknowledge their frustration with police unions and decry the limited scope of interest many unions bring to the discussion.

A primary task of the police chief is to identify strategies and methods that facilitate active support from the police union for the department's vision. Certainly police unions are required to support the needs of their membership and, in some cases, this interferes with the chiefs' efforts to develop a positive working relationship between police leaders and their unions. The police leader must identify the areas of interest that support both achieving the department's vision and the individual needs of the police officers. Although chiefs do strive to secure improved compensation packages, skills training, and better equipment for their officers, their primary goal should be gathering the resources necessary to support work of the department and engaging all officers directly in accomplishing the department's vision.

Many organizations in the private and public sectors are exploring leadership practices that empower and engage their workforce. The research around engaging employee commitment underscores the value of acknowledging and recognizing employees for a job well done. In the police culture, there are many opportunities to acknowledge the positive behavior of the individual line officers. Unfortunately, the lack of strong support for supervision within the police culture seems to facilitate condemning poor behavior rather than rewarding good work and positive outcomes. Chiefs who believe in a more constructive form of internal police politics recognize the value of their relationship with the officers and unions, and have begun to identify new methods for officer recognition and a more demonstrable level of support from the community. These steps help redefine a police culture that has focused on preventing the negative rather than rewarding the positive.

External Politics and Relationships with Other Partners

8

Police chiefs' visions impact not only their departments but also community and political leaders. William Bratton, in his book *Turnaround*, and Pat Murphy in *Commissioner* describe their relationships with their mayors and the impact of the political world on their ability to achieve their policing goals.[1] In many instances, a chief's tenure coincides with that of the mayor who has hired him or her. Because they serve in appointed positions, the ability of police chiefs to negotiate a productive relationship with the mayor is fundamental to their success.

The Chief's Relationship with the Mayor: Another Challenge of Leadership

Mayors appoint the majority of American police chiefs. The relationship between the chief and a city's mayor can be another area in which the police chief must create a balance that allows for addressing the department's priorities and those of the mayor. Police chiefs talk about the life span of their mayoral appointment as limited, in many cases to only 3 or 4 years. The relationship between the mayor and the police chief requires a commitment from both to a shared vision and to the strategies that must be implemented to reach the agreed upon goals. In many instances, chiefs' struggle with this relationship as both the community and the media can quickly identify the police chief as the city's primary leader, which can cause friction with the elected mayor. In some instances this high-visibility leadership role conflicts with the mayor who may feel threatened or undermined by the police chief's identification as the primary leader of a city or town. As the chiefs outline in the following discussion, the relationship with the mayor is pivotal to the success or failure of any American police chief.

Bratton talks about the length of his own tenures as a police chief and his relationship with two mayors. Bratton believes that his tenure in Los Angeles will require at least two 5-year terms. He also recognizes the limits of his New York City tenure under Mayor Giuliani, but balances the comment with his observations about his successor's ability to sustain the changes that he had introduced as commissioner.

> There's no ideal formula in terms of the timing for a chief. I think it's very situational dependent. For example, I'm going to stay between 5 and 10 years in

Los Angeles to institutionalize the changes that I think are necessary to reinstate the LAPD on its pedestal and keep it going without falling back. In New York City, ironically, after the 27 months I spent there the changes had been institutionalized. There's not a lot that happened after I left that was different from the changes made by me and my team. [Of course, the exception would be terrorism, where Commissioner Ray Kelly] is doing a phenomenal job as leader of that department and dealing with that new threat.

Situational leadership and tenure are both related to the chief's relationship with the mayor, as Bratton explains in his own case.

The length of time that a chief should be in place varies. Normally and ideally, it should be 3 to 5 years because after that they'll be waiting you out in the department. I've had good and bad relationships with the mayor and am a product of my experiences. I have had a better relationship with former Mayor James Hahn and now Mayor Villaragosa because of the tough relationships with Mayor Giuliani in New York and Mayor Menino in Boston. If I had stayed in Boston, I think that Mayor Menino and I would have worked out okay, but there would have been some rough patches as he is very hands-on, similar to Giuliani. Giuliani wanted to be in the police department managing day to day. This is the total anathema to my style of policing, which is picking good people and then holding them accountable for their work.

The best teams are when the mayor and police chief have similar styles of leadership. The Los Angeles mayor's leadership style is similar to my own. He wants to hire good people, he wants to be kept informed, and he wants no surprises, but day to day I don't hear from him. He has no role in selection of the personnel that report to me. Mayor Menino and Mayor Giuliani wanted to be involved with what should be the prerogative and responsibility of the police chief.

Bratton has done a good job at understanding the balance between the mayor and police chief's role. He has experienced both the positive and the negatives of the mayoral relationship. He is a leader who respects the needs of the mayor but also understands how to build a professional police organization. He is also committed to developing a police leadership team and organization that can be held accountable and responsible for its actions. He clearly understands the mandate of the mayor and also the limits of this authority that must be negotiated with the chief executive. The outcome of this negotiation equips the police chief with the scope of authority to do the job of police leader in a local community.

Charlotte–Mecklenburg, North Carolina, Police Chief Darrel Stephens has worked with many city mayors. He also offers wise counsel for police chiefs about developing working relationships with mayors.

I think the most important thing is to establish a relationship right off the bat where you have open lines of communication. You have a discussion about how you will handle a conflict right up front. There are probably going to be times when we disagree, and a lot of times there's something important that I don't understand and we have to have a conversation about that. The mayor may think that police officers can and should do certain things that are governed by law or criminal procedure, but we really can't do things differently unless the mayor changes the precedent or the law is changed. So we handle conflict and know what to do when we disagree.

Having that conversation actually puts mayors at ease. Some politicians keep the police at arm's length and don't want to be labeled as interfering with the police. Some don't care. A lot of them don't want to intervene in certain areas because they get a lot of feedback from the community and the police when they do. It's been my experience in every one of these conversations that you have to raise the issue of how to handle conflicts before they become public. It's in both the mayor's and the police chief's interest to do that up front.

Former Houston Mayor and Police Chief Lee Brown experienced both sides of this leadership equation. He has established many important benchmarks for police leaders, but also served three consecutive terms as the mayor of Houston. He emphasizes the importance of a close, working relationship between the mayor and the police chief.

As a police chief you have to establish a relationship with the mayor that is clear about the few things he wants to be advised on and what policies he wants to be involved in with the police department. You need to establish this up front and don't have the mayor read something in the paper without first hearing it from you. I think it's important for the chief to insist on meeting with the mayor weekly to ensure communication.

From the mayor's point of view, I want my chief to know that I'm not the chief, you're the chief and I expect you to run the department and I don't want any surprises. If there's a serious policy issue, then let's talk about it together and then you can implement it. However, as mayor, I am the one who will ultimately be responsible for policy in all city departments. As to the chief's longevity, it used to be 2 years and now it's 3, but the number one impact on the chief's tenure is political. A new mayor wants his or her own police chiefs. They want to pick their own person.

Brown and Stephens both suggest that an upfront understanding of how conflicts will be discussed will facilitate a smooth flow of communication between policy makers and police leaders. Of course, the mayor is the final decision maker about the vision and policy of the police department. With this in mind, White Plains, New York, Commissioner Frank Straub describes what might happen when a police chief's successful implementation of the department's vision undermines the relationship between the mayor and the police chief.

> The more you change successfully, the more attention you get, and the more attention you get, the more you're potentially in conflict with the mayor or city manager because now you're cutting into their ego and their space. It's like walking on a tightrope and you really have to walk it carefully. If you don't change enough, then you're screwed because they don't need you any more because you didn't do the job. If you change too much, now you're crossed over into someone else's political territory.
>
> In White Plains, the previous commissioner was never allowed to talk to the press. One of the things the mayor said when they hired me was they wanted me to be available and accessible to the press. I believed this too because it's important for the department to read about itself when things are going well. A good press relationship is also important when things turn bad; you have capital in the bank, so to speak, that you can build on in your interactions with the press. We were highly visible here with the press and did a lot of press stuff at City Hall, but all of a sudden City Hall started saying we couldn't talk to the press anymore. We had to get approval from the mayor's office. It's a weird thing because you have to be there with the press and the community, but by being there you can get in trouble.
>
> If you read Bratton's book, that's what got him in trouble with Rudy [Giuliani]. They hired Bratton and told him to drive down crime. He drove down crime and got the recognition, and then the mayor says he really was the one that drove down crime. At one time, Bratton almost became the face of New York City over Rudy. The police commissioner was saying one thing and the mayor was saying something else. So I think it's very hard not to burn out your relationship with whoever is the mayor and the longer you stay the more difficult it is to manage the relationship. Three or three and half years have become the shelf life for a police chief. I don't think there's anything you can do to avoid the conflicts; it just happens. You can get yourself into a hole, pull the top over, and sit there, but that's not good for organization.

In Commissioner Straub's 5-year tenure, the crime rate has been dramatically reduced and his innovative community policing approaches have made a significant impact on a variety of other issues, including domestic violence and youth-related crime. Nevertheless, he still must actively work to maintain a good relationship with the mayor.

Lessons Learned about the Relationship with Mayors

Richard Pennington, Atlanta's police chief, actually ran as a candidate for mayor of New Orleans after his police tenure. He was well known for addressing police corruption in New Orleans, so his understanding of the relationship between the mayor and police chief grows out of direct experience with some of the most serious challenges a police chief confronts in any community.

> The first thing that you have to do when you're working for a mayor is understand what the vision of the mayor is and the goals that the mayor has set for the city. Then you can never compromise your own position in relationship to these goals at anytime. I always tell chiefs that if you don't agree with something the mayor wants to do because it is unethical, then the best thing to do is resign because it's not going to work. If they do something unethical once, they will do it again a second time. I was lucky enough to work for Mayor Morial in New Orleans and Shirley Franklin here in Atlanta, and I've never had that problem. They have been the best two people that I ever worked for.
>
> I tell chiefs that working for a mayor is a "delicate" relationship because one day they love you and the next day they can hate you. A lot of it comes from the pressure that is put on them from the community. If all of a sudden you've got three or four brutality cases in a week or a month, people want to know what the police chief is doing about it. The pressure can come down just like that. I've seen chiefs get run out because of high-speed police chases. Let's say an officer gets into a high-speed police chase and kills innocent people. Then there's another chase and by the time the third one comes along the mayor will step in and say this chief is not doing something right and we're going to replace him. Just like that! Sometimes the unions put pressure on the politicians as well.

Pennington has faced some serious community confrontations in Atlanta, including controversial police shootings of suspected drug dealers and an older parent of one of the suspects. Still, he has developed close working relationships with a wide range of community leaders, including Atlanta's gay and lesbian community as well as new immigrant communities. The results of his efforts to build strong community relationships have enabled him to weather some tough community confrontations as well as to continue to enjoy the continuing support of the mayor.

Drew Diamond offers some candid, reality-based suggestions about working with the mayors of American cities. His ideas are based on both his Tulsa, Oklahoma, experience and extensive consulting experience with police chiefs.

> Get a contract. A lot of guys want to become police chiefs so bad that they won't push for a contract. They'll take it as it is and I've seen them last 90 days and get run out of town. Other than that, it's like any other relationship. The mayor and the police chief need to sit down and understand the dimensions of both roles.

The mayor needs to own every success of the police department. That's the reality. If the police department wants to own everything, that doesn't work. A strong police chief who is respected and well liked by the community and his department can survive those kinds of things. Emotionally sometimes it beats you up but you can get through it. I knew a major city police chief years ago who got his staff stripped and eventually left the job and went on to become chief in another major city. His mayor got irritated because the chief got on the cover of a national magazine for reducing crime in that city. The mayor thought he should have been on the cover. It was the magazine that made the call. They had pictures of both the chief and the mayor, but thought the catalyst for change was the police chief.

Now I've seen some big cities that have really good mayors who are not only supporting their police chiefs, but giving them direction in terms of the vision and the community. They're getting it right. I do a lot of work with mayors, city managers, and police chiefs all in the same room and problem solving together. I don't think a police chief can fix an incompetent mayor. I've watched police chiefs go quiet when they get stuck or think they have an incompetent mayor. Sometimes that's the best thing to do. I think it's a mistake when chiefs try to manipulate around their mayors, whether they're competent or incompetent, and go to the city council. They violate their own chain of command and that's a mistake. I've watched mayors try to go around their police chiefs and reach into their command staff or the union directly. That's wrong too, but they can do it, even when it's a violation of the city charter. When those things start happening, it's probably time to leave.

Diamond acknowledges that he made mistakes when he allowed his own ego to get in the way of building a strong, collaborative relationship with the mayor of Tulsa. He learned some tough lessons about leadership when he was confronted by his police union with a vote of confidence as well as intense scrutiny by both the local media and local city council. With these challenges in mind, Diamond reiterates the importance of building strong working relationships with political leaders and ensuring both public and private support of the police department's vision.

Diamond's long-time colleague, Robert Lunney, who has been police chief in Canada and an international consultant on police leadership, thinks police chiefs need to keep a low profile, which is itself a balancing act.

Police chiefs are not politicians but they have to have a good political sense. They have to have political skills. You have to speak to the public and lead the public and do all the things that politicians do. You have to show up on time and shake hands and be a good listener. Sometimes if you're in the media too often and it's too positive, the politicians get jealous. So you have to manage your public profile and make sure that you're not getting too prominent or that you're getting too much ink. So it's a balance there to make sure you're doing your job representing law enforcement and policing to the public and keeping a respectful profile of the politicians.

Leonard Hamm of Baltimore, Maryland, uses football as an analogy to describe his working relationship with the mayor.

> We are a football team. The mayor says he wants a Super Bowl championship, but he doesn't tell me how to get it. He doesn't tell me who will play what position in order to get the championship. I report directly to him everything we're doing, how we're spending the money and what our goals and objectives are. I solicit input from him to ensure that we're working his ideas and my ideas into the same goal. That's our relationship.

Though Hamm outlines a fine theoretical framework, he faced difficult political challenges when the mayor ran for governor. Suddenly, Hamm was confronted by political pressure to avoid any possible embarrassments that might impact the gubernatorial race. Though the mayor won the election, Hamm views their shared vision in a slightly different way.

> The mayor's idea was that enforcement or locking people up is the most important thing to do to reduce crime. I disagree with that approach. You have to have both enforcement and community relationships to solve other problems in the community. The fact that some say cops are not social workers is not true; we in fact are dealing with social issues all the time. We deal with many things that contribute to crime, such as education, economic woes, and health issues. I believe those issues have to be addressed, not necessarily by the police, but we can provide some support and assistance to those who do work on these issues. This is one way we can help reduce crime, other than arresting people.

Unfortunately, Hamm was confronted by another mayoral election immediately following the gubernatorial selection. The new mayor decided to address some of the social issues that plagued a significant portion of the city's population. She also decided to support Hamm's problem-solving approach in reducing crime. As he attempted to work collaboratively with the mayor, electoral politics and a rising murder rate cast a harsh shadow over his tenure, and he was replaced during the heat of the election season. Hamm promoted teamwork with the mayor, but never was able to build the necessary support for his vision that incorporated both strong enforcement and significant engagement of his police officers and the community. In addition, his vision of "partnering to prevent crime" with other city agencies, such as education, housing, and health, was never realized as the police department was continuously refocused by the mayor on the suppression of crime as its primary and only task.

Chief Dean Esserman is more provocative when he considers his own relationship with the city's mayor. He believes strongly that there can be serious consequences for not keeping a low profile and being a team player.

> Many police chiefs have become rock stars. There's a danger in that because they're the most visible person out there besides the mayor. When people ask me about the weather, I tell them what the mayor thinks of the weather. I think a mayor is frequently betrayed by his police chief as the chief's ego gets bigger. I am only part of the mayor's team and although I am proud to be a part of his team, I am only a part of his overall vision. I have no agenda of my own. The relationship is often tempestuous and even those that are based on good faith can turn bad. That's a danger because there is only one casualty and it will always be the police chief.

Esserman is a realistic police leader who understands the mandate of the chief and the mayor's overall authority for police services in a city. As chief of Providence, Rode Island, Esserman has been successful at demonstrating his commitment to the city, and his unswerving partnership and support for the mayor. In this case, he has modeled a relationship between the police chief and the mayor that works for both of them and has worked well for the city.

Finally, Wayne Tucker offers this assessment of his relationship with his first mayor, Jerry Brown, in Oakland, California. Tucker worked hard to build a strong relationship with Brown, though he did suggest that Brown mistakenly ventured into some operational territory, which caused problems for both of them.

> First, I think that it's important that I work very hard to be a good subordinate. I generally keep the mayor informed about what my issues are and where I want to go. I try to present my issues and make my decisions on his time. If I see resistance or conflict coming, I make sure that he knows in advance. I check off with him so that he understands my issues and where I'm coming from. Over the past year and a half, I've had no occasions in which he has directed me to do something or forbade me to do something, which is very encouraging. We've had a couple of contentious conversations over various issues, mostly the increasing crime rate and what's a doable response and what we can expect the outcome to be of the response. He has actually been reasonably deferential, which is a bit different than I've seen with other colleagues and their mayors.

As other chiefs, Tucker describes how to develop and sustain a working relationship with a mayor. A high level of regular communication is important as well as the classic "no surprises" approach to keeping the mayor informed of all bad news and challenging events that may confront the police and ultimately the mayor. The mayor is one of the primary external influences that all police chiefs must manage, but there are many other important community actors and political partnerships that have a direct day-to-day impact on the chief's success. The ability to balance these many relationships is one of the fundamental responsibilities of a police leader.

Watchdog Committees and Departmental Oversight

In some communities, political leaders have established external public oversight committees to monitor police officer behavior. Unfortunately, many grew out of situations that involved police corruption, as in the case of the Knapp Commission in New York City.[2] Other cities have developed oversight commissions to monitor citizen complaints and negative police behavior.

While some chiefs have found oversight committees to be supportive and believe that they have worked effectively with the department's internal affairs unit, others express concern about the meddling of these committees in the affairs of their departments. Drew Diamond has had to work with oversight committees in Tulsa and other places.

> First of all, I find almost none of them, and there are more than 60 operating across the country, have any great value or any real potential to change departments. One of two things happens during the civilian review process of the police department, no matter how they got started or no matter what their history. What happens is they [the civilian review board] either become "cop groupies," another layer of bureaucracy, or they basically slow down the internal processes, or they become so nasty about the issue and they become another arm of the investigation. Cops resist them and I don't blame them. It just never works to change the norms or the culture that got them in there in the first place. Communities reach for them because they don't know what else to reach for. When they get embattled, they get frightened and bad things happen. Those police departments deserve the oversight committees because they don't provide any alternative. The alternative is trust building with the community. I've seen police departments where officers have done ugly and violent things, but they don't even get sued because there's so much trust in the pocket. Nobody would suggest having a citizen review board because the community trusts the department and the chief. A good officer who makes a mistake can survive because of the trust in the department. I've watched it happen in my career.

Diamond is one of the most articulate, thoughtful proponents of the community policing model. Rightfully, he observes that introducing an oversight commission for a police department is a comment about the failure of both the police and the political leadership in a community. The responsibility for the oversight and accountability of police behavior ultimately sits with the mayor and a city's elected council members. The police chief also bears major responsibility for ensuring the police officers not only respect the law, but, more important, respect all members of the community. There is no doubt that oversight committees have been introduced to monitor and in some cases attempt to control, if not prevent, deviant police behavior. In some cases, this has been of value, but in most cases the watchdog groups are either marginalized by the police bureaucracy or their own inability to understand the necessity of keeping accountability within the functional political and organizational processes.

Robert Olson's assessment of the utility of oversight committees is also quite candid.

> This is where the reality is perception. I had one and, as long as I was the ultimate decision maker, I couldn't have cared less. I could lean on them. They took 2 years to do an investigation that I would complete in 90 days. The board sustainability rate on cases was only 6% and mine was 38%. It seemed that they did not want to work with our Internal Affairs department. The civilian review went on forever. It was so bad that I would get a case on a guy for the third time and other things he had done were still sitting in civilian review, so I couldn't use that as progressive discipline. I couldn't even fire him, even though he had done it three times and it was time to fire him under my matrix. It was a terrible problem. So I look at it as something to make someone happy politically, but it's not helpful. I think it stopped some firings that could have happened sooner.

Most chiefs feel that oversight boards undermine their management authority. They understand the political value of having community representation in the affairs of the police department, but the oversight board process is slow and ultimately chiefs believe it is their responsibility to manage their officers' behavior.

However, experienced chiefs have been able to work successfully with oversight committees when they are closely partnered with Internal Affairs units to expedite the process and ensure a clear determination of the facts in the case. It remains the role of the police chief to monitor, manage, and finally discipline the police officers for any behavior that is either illegal or clearly inappropriate. The failure of a police chief to accept this responsibility and develop a clear set of norms that disallow negative behavior will ultimately lead to the downfall of the chief. No external committee can alleviate the chief's responsibility for managing police officers' behavior. It seems more worthwhile for a chief to build relationships directly with the community rather than spending time building a process for monitoring, which may have little or no impact on police officers' behavior.

Police Chief Tucker worked with an oversight committee in Oakland. One of his primary mandates from the mayor was to make certain that the federal consent decree was implemented fairly to improve Oakland police officers' performance and behavior. He also had to deal with the community-crime-control councils, which continuously interfered with his deployment of police officers in local neighborhoods. Tucker had inherited a department that was attempting to move toward a community policing model, but was still essentially entrenched in the old professional model, with limited problem-solving competencies and a lackluster relationship with the community.

Tucker's relationship with the mayor was crucial to working with the oversight committee. The Community Policing Advisory Board had been pushing him hard to move the department into a more comprehensive approach to community policing strategies, but the board did not fully appreciate the department's ability to respond to those demands.

> They are all well intentioned and I don't think any of them wants anything but the best for this department. They are very passionate about what they're doing, but I think they are unrealistic about what they want us to do at this time in our history. With the resources the department has today, it's just not doable.

Tucker remained in his position during the transition from one mayor to another, which speaks volumes about how to maintain a relationship with a city mayor. Oakland's new mayor, Ron Dellums, has moved toward a community policing strategy while still emphasizing enforcement and reducing the crime rate.

Significance of the Working Relations with the Police Chief's Partners

The relationship between the mayor and the police chief must benefit both parties. Most successful chiefs have anticipated potential conflicts and worked with their mayors to establish a process for resolving their differences. Other chiefs acknowledge that their own mistakes have undermined developing a more compatible relationship. The ultimate decision maker is always the mayor, and all chiefs recognize their subordinate role in this partnership. However, chiefs must be comfortable with their own abilities to establish a clear vision for their officers, the police department, and the community. As Lunney points out, "the role of the police chief does have political dimensions and the police chief is a politician, for better or worse."

All police chiefs have strategies for working with the mayor. Many emphasize the value of establishing the relationship early in their tenure, recognizing that the mayor ultimately controls the use of resources and the resolution of both police and nonpolice issues. In fact, some mayors insist on staying directly involved with the day-to-day management of the police department, which can cause difficulties when the mayor and his or her staff spend an inordinate amount of time and energy directly engaged in police matters. The daily intervention from the mayor's office can make police chiefs feel their authority is being undermined and the entire department is being disempowered.

Oakland Police Chief Tucker experienced difficulties with his civilian oversight board and his neighborhood councils, both of which were trying to assess the appropriate allocation of police resources for Oakland's neighborhoods. Tucker finally drew the line and clarified their roles in relation to his role as the police chief. This type of conflict illustrates why police leaders need to be clear about the parameters of community involvement and how to develop collaborative partnerships.

The relationship between the police chief and the mayor may have clear time boundaries. Many mayors only serve one 4-year term or at most two consecutive terms. Thus the chief has a short time period in which to change the police culture, establish a clear vision, and implement this vision in the community. Chief Bratton recently received another 5-year contract with the Los Angeles Police Department. As Bratton described earlier, he thinks a 10-year tenure is needed to change the culture of the Los Angeles Police Department. Changing any organization in a 4-year period is uncertain, if not impossible. Still, police chiefs take on this challenge and make a Herculean effort to implement an organizational vision that supports the development of a safe, economically viable, and healthy community. The relationship with the mayor and other external political actors is fundamental to the success of this venture. Failure to recognize the importance of this relationship has led to the downfall of many police chiefs and probably a few mayors as well.

The Future of American Policing
Looking Back and Forward

9

Police chiefs face crises in their careers that are sometimes not of their own making. When Commissioner Leonard Hamm was ousted in the heat of a mayoral election, newspaper columnist Michael Olesker wrote a piece titled "Hamm's Ouster Does Little to Dent Social Miasma" in *The Baltimore Sun*.[1]

> Homicides are only the headline item. More and more kids are getting sucked into these gangs, which offer a sense of belonging they aren't getting at home. They also offer them better weaponry and better protection when they have to go behind bars. Does anybody think a police commissioner can offer the emotional security these kids need, and the loving parents, so these kids don't have to tell themselves gangs are the only place they can get some attention? We live in a city once divided by race that is now, more and more, divided by economics. We do ourselves a disservice when we focus strictly on crime. It is a fact of life, but our lives consist of more than crime. Hamm gave it his best shot. But there are places where a police commissioner can't go. One of them is inside of people's homes. Another is inside of their heads.

After reading Olesker's column, Commissioner Frank Straub of White Plains, New York, suggested that the "police are being held accountable for solving social ills." Unfortunately, as Olesker points out in his article, Hamm laments that a chief "can't do it for a host of reasons. One could argue that we have become our own worst enemy, [because of our] success in reducing crime, high accountability through Compstat, and many times [being] the only people with the clarity of vision and the willingness to try."

In this chapter, the chiefs reflect on their relationships with the community and their tenure as police chiefs. In addition, they offer observations about the future of policing and police leadership.

Reflections about Leadership and Change

Even when the chief has a vision, implementation is not always easy. In many cases, the vision of the chief clashes with the needs and demands of other governmental departments and community needs that do not relate directly to the police department's mission. Many obstacles confront police chiefs on

115

a daily basis as they shape their vision and mobilize their officers to implement it within the community.

David Couper, the longtime Madison, Wisconsin, chief and one of the pioneers of problem-solving policing, reflects on his tenure:

> After all these years as a police chief, and being such a renegade, PERF [Police Executive Research Forum] gave me the national leadership award. There were lots of chiefs who were younger than I was who saw things the same way I did and it was at that point that I felt that all of this has not been for naught. There are people out there who share the same ideas about the vital importance that an effective, honest police department with integrity can have in the life of a democracy.

Couper's reflection on his Herculean efforts to establish a credible, community-oriented police department deserves commendation. He was one of the earliest proponents of a new role model for a progressive police chief in American communities. He then offers this insight about his professional survival in Madison and his motivation for building a relationship with the community.

> I came into a department where I had a lot of experience and education and 4 years of experience as a chief in Burnsville [Wisconsin]. Even with this experience, a whole bunch of my Madison police officers said, we're not going to do this. To have rank-and-file officers sign a petition against me, it was like, what in the world is wrong? I thought I was one of you guys! I came into Madison thinking cops are cops. When I went into Burnsville, which was a small department of 14 officers, it was like, you're the chief now, and you're one of us, and let's try some stuff. In Madison, they didn't think I was one of them. I think that was a real shock but maybe that's the kind of shock that motivated me to say, look if you're going to survive around here, it's not going to be by getting every cop on your side, but it's going to be by getting the community to buy in to the ideas that you're talking about.

His biggest mistake was assuming that all of the officers were going to agree with his attitude that "Hey, we're all cops, so let's do this!" After a series of missteps, Couper realized that he had to focus on building consensus to support his vision. He describes the moment when he came to this conclusion.

> I remember going to a police union barbecue in the early summer of '73 or '74 and getting my kids out there and nobody talked to me. They shunned me. I've never been shunned by cops before and it shocked me. However, if I look back on it and if they had totally welcomed me and said this is the way we do things around here, but you're the chief now and we're really proud of

you, well maybe none of this improvement [problem-solving approaches and community policing] would have ever happened.

The power of the police culture can severely impact relationships with the community. However, good leadership can guide organizations in new directions that ultimately are beneficial to the departments and the community.

Robert Olson offers a wonderful woodworking analogy about leadership and the process of change, based on a paper on change management that he and Robert Lunney wrote for PERF in the mid-1980s.[2]

> The job of the police chief is to take a stick of wood and make it into an arch. If you work with the wood, you take a stick and plant it firmly, which is traditional policing, and you grab hold of the top and rub it with lemon seed oil and you have to keep constant pressure on it. Leadership is about applying pressure. As you're applying pressure, you have to listen to its creaks and groans, knowing full well that if you don't put enough pressure on it, it's not going to bend and if you put too much pressure on it, it's going to break. You listen and you rub and you listen and you rub and you end up with an arch! I made some mistakes in Corpus Christi [Texas] because I was naïve; I had been deputy chief and I moved too fast for the culture. What I was doing was right, but how I was doing it was wrong. I didn't listen to the creaks and groans as I should have and I broke it.

Olson's analogy describes an accurate picture of the sensitivity and steady commitment that must be central to the police chief's efforts to establish a vision and then carefully craft its implementation both within the department and the community. His analogy incorporates both the thoughtful skills of the craftsperson and, possibly of greater importance, the tremendous patience and listening skills of a wise organizational leader. To Olson's credit, he shares his own critique of his failures in Corpus Christi, but his subsequent successes as a chief indicate that he learned many lessons from his earlier experiences.

At 38, Joe McNamara was the youngest police chief in America at the time of his appointment in 1973 in Kansas City, Missouri. He stayed there for less than 4 years, but went on to serve as the chief of San Jose, California. Bill Landsdowne, now of San Diego, served as a senior commander for McNamara in San Jose and offers this sad commentary on the extent of recognition and acknowledgment chiefs receive for their leadership and vision for change.

> The San Jose police department in 1974 was out of control. We could do just about anything that we wanted and there was no concept of the community. We were very aggressive back then. Joe came in and made several changes. One was to bring women into the organization, which was a very hard sell.

He got a vote of no confidence his first year because he disciplined an officer for using profanity in an arrest where he shouldn't have used it. We were just appalled, as that's what we did all the time. He created diversity in the police department and believed in the community. He instituted community liaisons, changed the training, selected the right people for promotions, people who thought and believed like he did. The example I'll give you, and it still rings in my mind, is that we had a Christmas party in San Jose every year and we were all there one year when they said, "I'm sorry that Chief McNamara can't be here but his wife is here." Everybody stood up and cheered and clapped. It was terrible. All those things that he did and the changes that he made in that organization cost him personally. Still it made San Jose the fine police department that it is today.

McNamara sadly remembers his loneliness as a police leader and the fact that he never had any friends in the department. He feels that was probably the fate of any police leader who attempted the dramatic changes that he accomplished in San Jose. Like Joe McNamara, Charles Gain successfully brought a new orientation to Oakland, California, in the late 1960s that made a tremendous impact in the city as well as on the national dialogue about the future role of policing. He was a lonely, isolated leader who was celebrated externally for his vision, but unfortunately disdained by his own rank-and-file officers as an autocratic visionary.

The visions of chiefs and their predictions for the future of policing often reflect the mentors who influenced their own leadership development. George Napper, the former Atlanta police chief and University of California, Berkeley criminology graduate, based his efforts to bring his police department closer to the community in direct contrast to the negative model that had been presented since the 1950s by Chief William Parker of the Los Angeles Police Department. Napper was very concerned about the isolation of the Atlanta Police Department from its community and spent many years trying to make certain that it did not mirror the old LAPD model.

The Atlanta PD felt like an occupying force in the community and that was the problem. The movement has been away from that and we now understand the difficulties that being isolated and away from those people that cops end up spending the most time with [meaning the community].

I wanted the department to find in me an extension of who I am. Even when I was working my way through college, I would spend time tutoring at the YMCA. I was also a community organizer for almost 3 years. That's the kind of person that I am. I love people. I hate to see people screwed over; that bothers me. I will not tolerate it when police officers abuse their authority to take advantage of people. It sickens me. I still have many problems with the police. When I think about police officers the image is not as positive as I would like it to be because I still see too much crap that goes on with recruiting your own people into the department. I think you have to understand the larger picture of life and be engaged in it in ways that really count for the community.

Napper clearly understands the challenge of bringing a police department and the community together. His personal experiences working in the community underscore his understanding of the difficulties that he encountered as he attempted to take the Atlanta Police Department out of its "fortress" mentality. Napper is not alone in his observations about the relationship between the police and the community. Police chiefs have shared these observations but still face the same challenges that Napper encountered to overcome the distrust and humiliation that some members of the community feel when confronted by the police in their communities.

Richmond, California, Police Chief Chris Magnus talks about the longevity of a police chief and sustaining change over the long term of the chief's tenure and the life of the department.

> I think being a chief is very seductive in terms of power and the influence. It's really hard not to get caught up in this racket. You sort of lose focus and think that the real measure of your success is when you're picked to do it somewhere that is bigger or better or different than where you are now. I think most chiefs have pretty healthy egos. This is a job where you don't get a lot of ego support from within or from the outside either. So one of the ways that your ego gets validated is knowing that you're wanted somewhere else and then focusing on the next job. That's not a problem if your goal is just career climbing. To me, it's hard because I see how long it takes to get everything done. If you're really trying to do this stuff, I don't know how you can do it in 3 years.
>
> I work closely with the community and the city government. But the biggest fear that I have here is that the community patience level is so fragile now. The community is frustrated. Their fear level and their disappointment and anger over past things are so high. I hope the department and I will be given a chance to be successful by doing things that take time to do right. These are changes that don't happen over 6 months or a year. My challenge is to find ways to show some short-term victories and accomplishments to show that progress is being made, so that people can feel like this is exciting and that there's something happening. At the same time, they need to understand that the kind of transformation that needs to occur here can't possibly happen as quickly as they would like it to. Murders are happening at the exact same clip as when I came here 6 months ago. I know people in the community are saying, What's up with that? I thought we were bringing this guy in to solve our violent crime problem and it seems like these homicides are happening all the time.

Magnus clearly presents the pressing challenge of a new chief who must quickly demonstrate the success of his vision. His effort to build a new relationship between the community and the police department is one of his

greatest challenges. He is also well aware that creating this trusting, productive relationship will take time to build. He also recognizes that it is absolutely
pivotal to the reduction of crime and the level of violence in the community.
His statement expresses an astute understanding of how a chief's personal
career agenda may not coincide with the timing to complete the task of creating this critical, new collaboration.

Current and Future Challenges

Recruiting new officers continues to be a challenge. There is consensus about
the value of higher education in the professional development of their officers,
but not all chiefs are convinced that a college education should be an entry-
level requirement. Police leaders are still exploring the best ways to work
with and mobilize community support for the police. They must constantly
strive to maintain a balance between enforcement strategies and respect for
the needs of local community members. There is concern about the lack of
national financial resources for the future development of the police institution. Finally, police chiefs are concerned about a rise in youth violence,
the impact of demographic changes in their communities, and the linger-
ing impact and responsibility for the prevention of terrorism throughout
the nation. These are some of the most pressing challenges that police leaders have discussed publicly and privately in the past few years. With this in
mind, police chiefs are now actively offering their observations about future
police leadership and specific suggestions that can impact both crime reduction and the role of the police in a democratic society.

Chief Darrel Stephens, of the Charlotte–Mecklenburg (North Carolina)
Police Department, has a number of concerns about the prospects for police
leadership in the future.

> Actually I'm a little worried about the future because I think we've got-
> ten a little bit confused over the past few years with the enforcement ver-
> sus community policing and problem-solving work. What concerns me is
> the type of approach we should take to policing issues, and how terrorism
> and our response to that fit into our whole democratic framework for polic-
> ing. Where does technology fit? Technology has had an enormous impact
> on policing in mostly positive ways. But it could be used in ways that we
> wouldn't expect it to. So right now I'm kind of confused about what the
> future is going to be about.

He fears that police officers are only being trained as managers rather
than future leaders. He worries about the counting of numbers and the
inability of chiefs to create a vision that really incorporates all members of the

community in a productive, crime-prevention strategy. He also recognizes that introducing new methods can impact the vision in both positive and potentially negative ways, and it takes time to manage and sustain change.

> It does worry me and it's always been a problem not just for policing but across the board. It's hard to help frame that vision or to stick with that vision for any substantial period of time if you want to accomplish something. In Police leadership, we're still in a position where in large cities, chiefs are going in 3 or 4 years. It's hard to sustain things.

Raleigh, North Carolina, Police Chief Jane Perlov has clear ideas about teaching future police leaders to carry out community-oriented policing.

> The community is getting more and more involved with policing. With the whole *CSI* [television series] phenomenon, people are much more interested in what we do now. They're taking much more of an active role and I think that's something that we need to figure out better, especially how we do it. Again, how we really involve the community, not just how we say that we involve them. It's a challenge for me now and I think it's going to get harder and harder. More people are going to get involved and you have a lot of old-fashioned police chiefs and you have a lot of new-thinking chiefs. Some of us have the advantage of using outside scholars, but it's a really hard thing to do.

Lee Brown is more concerned about the lack of innovation in policing.

> I don't hear anything that is really changing things. We've only had three primary changes in policing. We had the political era, then you had the revolution and reform era, and now we're in the community policing era. I just don't see the momentum to make sure that this sticks around. I'd like to see community policing become the dominant style of policing for all police agencies. As I said, it's grossly misunderstood, as most agencies say they have a form of community policing, but I don't see that happening.

Unfortunately, Brown has correctly assessed the state of police leadership and its commitment to the development of community policing. Many departments have created community policing goals, but have limited their implementation to specific units of their departments. Chiefs continue to struggle with the overall implementation of a community policing approach. They get lost in the arrest-and-enforcement mode of operation and find themselves reacting to negative community comments about overzealous police officers. In many cases, chiefs express the value of a community relationship with the police department but really have difficulty creating a tangible community partnership. In some cities, chiefs are confronted by a serious challenge for the police and local prosecutors as inappropriate police tactics have alienated local community members and created a lack of support for the police on the streets and in the courtrooms.

Lunney has worked extensively with PERF and the Police Corps, and is both optimistic and fearful about police leadership in the future.

> After a bit of a trough, we've got a good, skillful cadre of police chiefs coming into their own now. I see them being proactive, aggressive, vigorous, and more achieving. I also see them as having tools that are superior to what we had in the past and I see them working with the tools. However, terrorism and the national security situation are going to make it very difficult to adhere in an idealistic way to those democratic principles from an earlier era. I fear for local policing in this era and I share this viewpoint with the PERF leadership. We're getting a familiar rise in crime rates. That's what happened in the 1970s and early 1980s. You can see that crime wave coming back. I don't see the government willing to infuse the police with the necessary resources to deal with it. The United States federal government has taken money out of Department of Justice programs and put it into homeland security. In Canada, the government never supported local policing to the extent that they did in the U.S. We're going to get hurt because of that, without the benefit of research and the applied research that we had in the past. So I see the security situation and the terrorist emergency situations as being a problem for all of the chiefs. I think it will be difficult for chiefs to sustain democratic principles in the face of this pressure.

Lunney understands the delicate balancing act that police chiefs must manage as they face new security challenges while trying to build and maintain good relationships in their communities.

Chief Ron Davis of East Palo Alto, California, who is a first-time chief, offers this advice to future police leaders.

> I think they have to have a very realistic assessment of what being a police chief is all about. They have to realize that a police chief in this century has to be a good technician, tactician, and consensus builder, and has to really like people. There has to be a good fit with the community too, especially for a first-time chief. I think I'm a good fit for East Palo Alto, whereas somewhere else it would be a total nightmare. If you lie in the wrong bed, you'll wake up and wish you never took the job.

Superintendent Rick Fuentes of the New Jersey State Police warns that police leaders have to be immersed in organizational learning, the community environment, and even the latest social and technological research.

> A police leader has to know his environment although he's sitting in the office. Some may say it's an ivory tower, but they have to know the environment their organization works in. The accountability demanded by the community

pushes that orientation. There is no isolating a police leader any more. The police leader is responsible for what goes on in the organization. I think the future police leaders will have to be technologically astute. We've got new systems like a performance management system under the consent decree, and now that I've seen them work, I can't think of operating without them. I think police organizations are going to become very technical. They will essentially be their own think tanks. They are becoming more and more imbued with intellect. Police leaders can't simply sign off on patrol changes but instead need to think about new initiatives and taking them across the chain of command, so that intellect and knowledge are shared across the organization.

Fuentes addressed serious internal issues, such as racial profiling, by introducing performance management systems that technically linked supervisors to almost every operation of line police officers. Though this had some strong advantages, it also challenged the culture and norms of the organization. He has worked diligently to provide a new direction for the department and has been fortunate to receive considerable validation from both external and internal constituents for his efforts.

Ellen Hanson brings the discussion of the future of policing back to the basics. Though Hanson is chief in a small Midwestern department, she has been very involved in national leadership forums and is particularly interested in police recruiting and developing a future officer candidate pool.

Future police leaders are going to have to be better at cooperating with each other and other organizations in their communities. In addition, because we're going to have hiring challenges, we have to be careful that we don't lower our standards. So when someone says to me, "I have 20 job openings and I can't find anyone to fill them so I need to lower the bar," this possibility scares me. I think keeping our standards and our message clear is of critical importance to the future.

Clearly Chief Hanson has outlined an important concern of many police chiefs who are worried about maintaining and developing strong professional standards for police officers. Again, this is a central concern for police chiefs who recognize the future challenges of policing as well as the need to recruit talented police officers who can perform as future leaders. The Police Corps established a rigorous set of recruitment standards and strong community policing-oriented training programs. Unfortunately, that program was terminated by the Bush administration, along with many other police research and development programs.

The lack of budget support for developing new police approaches and significant research efforts is a significant concern for Seattle Police Chief Gil Kerlikowske.

Chiefs need to think about terrorism and developing their own understanding of affinity groups and how to balance civil rights issues with the reality of new immigrant populations. They also have to be aware of new crime categories, such as the Internet and elder abuse and financial exploitation. The research says that children of immigrants are not problem kids, but I worry about a second generation that is disenfranchised and doesn't have a stable family unit. Unfortunately, these kids will be headed for problems in our communities. I'm concerned that federal government supported research is so limited. The government is not funding longitudinal research to see if systems actually work or, worse, if they could possibly cause more problems. The role of the federal government is to provide solid research about what works and what doesn't, and put that information in the hands of policy makers in a timely fashion. There's nothing going on at the Department of Justice; it's all about terrorism. I think we're going to pay the price in the long run for not funding research and technology. To think that we put tasers [an electronic, theoretically, nonlethal weapon] in the hands of police officers and the only quality control for a taser is what the manufacturers tell you. The federal government should have been testing tasers.

Prior to his role as Seattle's chief, Kerlikowske was the deputy director of the federal government's COPS office, which provided much of the technical, research, and training support for police agencies from throughout the country. He has focused on policing issues related to immigration, juveniles, and technology. Though Kerlikowske has identified some of the key issues for policing, he clearly understands that the overall role of a police leader will require a greater flexibility as well as willingness to explore new innovations in policing. With this in mind, it remains evident that the role of the police and its relationship with the community will be a central theme for police leaders in the coming years.

Many chiefs are concerned about the lack of federal government support for local efforts to build a strong community policing capacity. In the 1990s, there was considerable financial support for local police departments, including federal funding for 100,000 new police officers as well as research and innovative police programs. With the advent of the Homeland Security Department and the post-9/11 political environment, the majority of this local police funding has been transferred to the Iraq war and counterterrorism support.

Los Angeles Police Chief William Bratton still believes in the need for empowering police officers to do community policing, however, he has moved toward a new intelligence-led model to policing. This model relies on intelligence data to identify potential criminals before they commit serious crimes. Bratton has also used this model for police intervention to prevent terrorism within the United States. Even as he has made this adjustment, he still must work with the Los Angeles community, which continues to demand a more sensitive, respectful police force. Bratton describes his vision for police officers working in communities.

> Very simply we are saying, look, I trust you to go out and police this city. But I'm going to hold you accountable. If you're corrupt, brutal, or racist, I'm going to find out about it. I'm going to fire you and I'm going to jail you if it's corruption. Other than that I'm going to empower you. I want you to go out and make arrests and be assertive. I want you to enforce the law, but I also want you to be aware about what is going on in the community. There are huge differences in the communities here. What are some of the community's priorities other than just traditional crime? If it's graffiti, we'll focus on those entities that deal with graffiti. If it's abandoned cars, then work with the traffic department to get rid of the abandoned cars. If it's prostitution, then find effective ways to deal with prostitution that won't alienate the community.
>
> We have to hold officers accountable for their power. It's about decentralization. It's about inclusion rather than exclusion. Police departments tend to be exclusionary and it's the case here in Los Angeles more so than any other department in America. We'll take care of it. You, the community, you stay over there. You and the rest of American law enforcement, well, we don't have to send anybody to see what you're doing because we have all of the answers. We're not going to share what we're doing because we're going to be sued along with you if something goes wrong. The mentality in Los Angeles was amazing in some respects.

Bratton confronts the history of Los Angeles policing and its lack of including the people of the city. Bratton understands police power and has worked diligently to hold his officers accountable for their actions. He has faced challenges in the community, as he has made some false starts with community inclusion as well as observed some of his officers demonstrate a complete failure of leadership. Still, he has maintained a strong set of community values that underscore his commitment to community policing. Though he has not been completely successful in the implementation of this vision, he has worked hard at building a new level of accountability for policing in Los Angeles. Bratton's candor, commitment to change, and overall willingness to hold himself accountable have established a new set of norms for police leadership. These characteristics of leadership are both admirable and important to the profession's present and future standing in this democracy.

What It Takes to Be a Successful Police Leader

Bratton is probably the leading advocate for developing a professional police leadership program.

A successful leader is first somebody that's going to set goals that even he or she is going to be measured by. Those goals have a significant amount of risk involved with them. You can't be risk adverse; you basically have to be risk focused. With those goals, you then work with your senior management to set up strategies to address them. As you move further down the food chain, then you create an environment where your captains and lieutenants have empowered your police officers with tactics to carry out strategies that will realize the goals of the organization. That's where the inclusion component comes in. You centralize and include as many people as possible in the thought process about how we meet the goals of the department, and then you hold them accountable for the power you give away to them.

Although technology and accountability are important, Bratton recognizes the value of empowerment to ensure that all officers are directly engaged in delivering the chief's vision for the department. In fact, he continues to face resistance to his community policing vision among his officers in Los Angeles. Although he is concerned about the difficulties of changing his department's culture, he remains optimistic about the future of policing and the potential for eventually building a strong, positive relationship with all members of the Los Angeles community.

As former president of the National Organization of Black Law Enforcement Executives (NOBLE), Chief Richard Pennington of Atlanta is already examining what police leaders will need in the future.

A police chief is going to have to have good human relations skills and is going to have to be educated, even more that we require now. In addition, new employees coming into the organization will be different than ones that joined the force 10 years ago. You're going to have a lot of employees that are technologically savvy and know how to manipulate technology. So the chiefs of tomorrow will have to be astute and stay up to date on technology.

Chiefs are going to have to ensure that they understand the dynamics of every neighborhood they serve, as well as the political process, because if they don't understand that they won't be chief for very long. On top of that, they need to understand that they will be measured in terms of effectiveness. Some chiefs figure that once they get selected they can just sit at their desk and take calls. At some point they'll learn quickly that they're responsible for the safety of our cities. Communities are going to give them resources and then when they say they're going to bring crime down, they're going to hold them to it.

Pennington's comments are accurate. He understands that the role of the police leader continues to evolve, but he also acknowledges that the chief must be prepared to be held accountable for specific goals such as crime reduction and the overall safety of the community. The need for more educated police leaders is a key component of an evaluation of 1,500 Police Corps graduates who are now working in police departments across the country. The study examined the impact of the innovative recruit training on the service experience of frontline police officers. The results provide insights on the positive value of a college education as a recruitment standard as well as the impact of the community-oriented police training offered through the Police Corps academies. Because many chiefs have promoted community policing, they may be able to incorporate lessons learned from the evaluation and identify training strategies to support their visions for local police services.

As police leaders debate the issue of professional education, the entire concept of lifelong learning has emerged as a new idea within the police community. Police leaders as well as military leaders have recognized that the world is changing, and it is critical that police leaders continue to develop and learn throughout the professional careers. Chief Drew Diamond of Tulsa, Oklahoma, has some interesting suggestions about required reading material for future police chiefs.

> I would tell them to read anything in the past 8 or 10 years written by the Dalai Lama. He's written some very short, thoughtful books about peacekeeping, peace, and how to treat others. I'm very influenced by the Dalai Lama. Most of the other leadership books talk about "making a list, doing seven things, and creating a cult around you." I find important ideas in classical writers and contemporary stuff that's becoming classical, such as Gandhi's writing, which is fascinating. Malcolm X's book had a big influence on me, in terms of how to promote transition and change. They were real fundamental, philosophical changes and the way he saw human beings helped me understand what I was trying to do as a police chief.

He then offers a somber assessment of some of the challenges ahead for police leaders.

> I think about the new challenge of working with the new immigrant populations and it will be about how American policing resists going back to a war model. Those departments that have institutionalized some levels of transparency in their community policing are going to fight to maintain it and I hope they do. I don't think there are going to be many new initiatives to get to that point, but I just don't want to lose the ones that are working now. There are people in this country who are pushing ideas that will make us become fearful, divisive, and ugly, and policing will begin to reflect that.

Chief Diamond and Chief Kerlikowske are concerned about the lack of comprehensive support for the development of future police initiatives from the federal level. Still both share a sense of optimism about the future, as they express their continuing commitment to community policing and the balancing act chiefs have to perform to ensure backing from the community for the work of their police officers.

This study has offered many of America's police chiefs the opportunity to tell their stories and express their opinions about what it takes to be a successful police leader. The lessons learned by the 26 police chiefs should serve any future police leader well. Police chiefs that incorporate some of the suggestions in this study could even insure their own success in the ever-changing political, departmental, and community environments they will encounter every day they are on the job.

With this in mind, it is appropriate to remember an observation from Mark Twain in *Life on the Mississippi* about the life of a riverboat pilot:

> Two things seemed pretty apparent to me. One was, that in order to be a [Mississippi River] pilot a man had got to learn more than any one man ought to be allowed to know; and the other was, that he must learn it all over again in a different way every twenty-four hours.

This may be the most realistic description of the life of an American police chief.

Recommendations for Police Chiefs and All People Interested in Supporting a Democracy 10

American police chiefs are a unique group of leaders committed to confronting some of the most difficult challenges in a democratic society. They have outlined their successes, their dilemmas, and their own approaches to devising and implementing a vision to meet the challenges. Although they recognize and uphold democratic values, they have also witnessed the difficulty of providing police services in a diverse set of communities, which demands a wide range of police sensibilities. All of the stories of the police chiefs in this study clearly suggest a number of recommendations that can be invaluable for present and future police chiefs in the United States.

1. A police chief must have a vision for the department. Don't surprise your staff, but build consensus to gain their support for the vision. Be prepared to explain the vision over and over and over again. The vision is the guiding light for everything the police will do in the community. The role of the leader is to explain it, reinforce it, and embrace it throughout his or her tenure with the department and the community.

2. A police chief should take time to analyze and diagnose problems in the community and the department. Be prepared to move quickly on some initiatives, but also have the patience to educate, nurture, and develop a vision that engages the entire department and promotes strong collaboration with the community. This is not an easy task; it requires strong communication skills and an ability to confront and overcome obstacles on a daily basis.

3. Police departments, like all organizations, have their own culture and internal norms. The chief must understand and be able to build on the departmental culture's strengths and eradicate its weaknesses. The norms dictate the way the department really operates. The chief must be prepared to address negative norms, build support for positive norms, and establish a new set of standards that promote achieving the department's vision. This also takes time, patience, and, again, outstanding communication skills.

4. Police chiefs must build a strong team of leaders to support the department's vision. Some chiefs have made mistakes by promoting their friends or allies instead of people who can effectively do the job. The team should be representative of all of the department's

129

interests and willing to work together. William Bratton's commitment to developing police leaders has been exemplary. He has begun to establish a leadership training model that accentuates the many lessons of leadership outlined in this study. Though there is a lot of chatter about leadership and management training, many of these training programs are tactically oriented and do not really focus on the reality of being a police chief in a democratic society. There is a critical need for leadership training that incorporates the lessons learned by the chiefs who participated in this study.

5. Encouraging and facilitating police officers and managers to buy in to the department's vision is a fundamental role of a police chief. Some chiefs have focused on ensuring that sergeants and lieutenants feel empowered and supported in their efforts to guide their officers. The value of these supervisors increases with good leadership training, which enables them in turn to build a strong, committed cadre of line police officers. Most current training for police supervisors is limited to administration and paperwork. Training should emphasize developing staff, dealing with personnel conflicts, and encouraging relationships between police officers and the community. Police supervisors must be able to give their street officers tools to make them more effective when working with the local community.

6. George Hart's story about involving police officers from New York City as interns in his department illustrates the importance of constructive feedback. This is an excellent example of how departments can share their experiences to support positive change. Similar internship opportunities and information sharing need continuing support. Federal financing has been severely restricted, so pressure to reinstate resources to support information sharing will be critical to future police leadership development.

7. The question about the appropriate tenure for a police chief and the amount of time necessary to foster significant change is complicated. David Couper had a 20-year tenure as a result of a contract created by the Wisconsin legislature. He could not be fired for anything other than a serious criminal or ethical violation. Most chiefs decry the current 3- to 4-year average longevity for police leaders, which severely limits their ability to have an impact even when they have the support of the mayor. San Francisco Chief Heather Fong and Miami Chief John Timoney offered searing critiques of the civil service system, which prevents identifying and promoting leaders based on talent rather than seniority. Basing tenure on performance does present a challenge to the police chiefs. First, they need to recognize the importance of their relationship with the mayor. In addition, they also must outline clear performance measures and a vision

that builds consensus both within the mayor's office and the community. This challenge is paramount to any police chief's survival and success.

8. This study was originally written as a doctoral thesis project for the University of California, Berkeley. At one time, the university had a prestigious School of Criminology that fostered developing some of this country's most distinguished police chiefs. Some of the chiefs have been included as participants in this book. Many of the chiefs interviewed for this book discussed the need for chiefs to have a broader view of life in their communities and our world. They also suggested that understanding the wider context of political and social life impacts the role of the police leader, and perspective will be essential to the success of future leaders. One of the chiefs suggested that all chiefs should not only read history, political science, and great literature, but also the Dalai Lama. The idea of lifelong learning is a fundamental concept of many leadership schools, including the United States Marine Corps. It has also become a key issue within the circle of police chiefs who are concerned about police leadership development. Many of the schools that prepare police officers are primarily technical colleges that teach police science and police tactics. Unfortunately, little attention is paid to the broader theoretical and societal issues that do and will impact police leaders. With these observations in mind, one of the major universities in this country should establish a police and criminal justice school that provides a leadership development curriculum that meets the needs of this field's future leaders. The school should offer the best instructors as well as an intellectual and practical leadership development context that can prepare this nation's police chiefs. Programs like the Police Corps should be expanded to encourage the recruiting of a high caliber of police recruits who will be prepared for a leadership role in policing. The federal and state governments should support this effort. It is critical to the future development of American police leadership.

9. Police chiefs need to implement specific activities that embrace accountability and empowerment of their officers and collaboration with the local community. The Compstat model promotes accountability and careful monitoring of police performance. It would be useful to include the community in the Compstat process as it offers a clear perspective on how to work cooperatively with the local police departments. Some chiefs have already begun to implement community involvement in the Compstat process as part of a partnership approach to policing.

10. Police chiefs need to examine their own commitment to community policing and the opportunities it offers to both the departments and

the community. Strong community partnerships through youth programs, community councils, and business groups establish important contacts and support that can help the department achieve its
goals and contribute to the longevity of the police chief's tenure.

The police chiefs' stories reinforce the fundamental need to have a clear
vision about their role in a democracy and the balancing act required to perform successfully. All have clearly experienced this challenge and in some
cases successfully implemented their visions. In other cases, they have failed,
but fortunately all understand why they have failed, and what they might do
differently in the future.

This study was designed to give 26 American police chiefs the opportunity to answer some fundamental questions about police leadership. They
graciously offered insights about their experiences, and shared the joy and
pain that every police chief has experienced on a regular basis. Most important, they celebrated the many challenges of working in a democracy, partnering with communities, and mobilizing their officers' support for their
vision. It is hoped that this study has captured both the difficulties and successes of police chiefs throughout the United States.

Notes

Introduction

1. Ronald A. Heifetz and Marty Linsky, *Leadership on the line*, Harvard Business School Press, Boston, 2002.

Chapter 1

1. Jerome Skolnick and James Fyfe, *Above the law: Police and the excessive use of force*, Free Press, New York, 1993, pp. 184–186.
2. Robert Reiner, *Chief constables*, Oxford University Press, Oxford, 1991, pp. 10–11.
3. Skolnick and Fyfe, *Above the law,* pp. 47–49.
4. Kerner Commission: National Advisory Commission on Civil Disorder, U.S. Government Printing Office, Washington, DC, 1968.
5. George Kelling, *The Kansas City preventive patrol experiment: A summary report,* Police Foundation, Washington, DC, 1974.
6. Ibid.
7. Ibid.
8. James Q. Wilson and George L. Kelling, Broken windows, *The Atlantic,* 249, no. 3 (March 1982): 29–38.
9. David C. Couper and Sabine H. Lobitz, *Quality policing: The Madison experience,* Police Executive Research Forum, Washington, DC, 1991.
10. William Bratton, *Turnaround*, Random House, New York, 1998, pp. 233–239.
11. James Q. Wilson, *Bureaucracy*, Basic Books, New York, 1989, pp. 37–38, 67–68.
12. William Ker Muir, Jr., *Police: Streetcorner politicians*, University of Chicago Press, Chicago, 1979.
13. Lou Cannon, *Official negligence: How Rodney King and the riots changed the LAPD*, Westview, Boulder, CO, 1999.
14. Todd Wuestewald, Brigette Steinheider, and Petra Saskia Bayeri, *From the bottom up: Sharing leadership in a police agency* [Abstract], paper presented at Berkeley Center for Criminal Justice Forum, Berkeley, CA, October 2006.
15. Wilson, *Bureaucracy.*
16. George Kelling, *The Kansas City preventive patrol experiment: A summary report,* Police Foundation, Washington, DC, 1974.
17. See William A. Geller, *Police leadership in America: Crisis and opportunity,* American Bar Foundation, Chicago, 1985, on private security including Michael Shanahan's "Private Enterprise and the Public Police: The Professionalizing Effects of a New Partnership."

Chapter 2

1. William Bratton, *Turnaround*, Random House, New York, 1998.

Chapter 4

1. Herman Goldstein, *Problem-oriented policing*, McGraw Hill, New York, 1990.

Chapter 5

1. President Johnson's Commission on Law Enforcement and the Administration of Justice, 1967.
2. George Kelling, *The Kansas City preventive patrol experiment: A summary report*, Police Foundation, Washington, DC, 1974.
3. James Q. Wilson and George L. Kelling, Broken windows, *The Atlantic*, 249, no. 3 (March 1982): 29–38.
4. Egon Bittner, The police on skid-row: A study of peace keeping, *American Sociological Review*, 32, 699–715, 1967.
5. Ibid.

Chapter 6

1. President Johnson's National Advisory Commission on Civil Disorders, the Kerner Commissioner Report, 1967.

Chapter 7

1. Wesley G. Skogan, Why reforms fail, Center for Criminal Justice's Conference on Empowerment of Police, University of California at Berkeley, Fall 2006.
2. Hans Toch, Douglas Grant, and Raymond T. Galvin, *Agents of change*, John Wiley and Sons, New York, 1975.

Chapter 8

1. William Bratton, *Turnaround*, Random House, New York, 1998; Patrick V. Murphy and Thomas Plate, Patrick Murphy, *Commissioner: A view from the top of American law enforcement*, Simon & Schuster, New York, 1977.
2. Report of the Commission to Investigate Allegations of Police Corruption and the Anti Corruption Procedures (Knapp Commission), 1974.

Chapter 9

1. Michael Olesker, Hamm's ouster does little to dent social miasma, *Baltimore Sun*, July 23, 2007.
2. Robert Olson and Robert Lunney, *Change management*, unpublished manuscript, Police Executive Research Forum (PERF), 1980.

Suggested Reading

Abrashoff, Michael D. (2002). *It's your ship*. New York: Warner Books.

Bakal, Yitzhak. (2005). *Normative leadership*. Paper presented at the North American Family Institute Annual Conference, Danvers, MA.

Bardach, Eugene. (1998). *Getting agencies to work together*. Washington, DC: Brookings Institution Press.

Barnard, Chester I. (1938). *The functions of the executive*. Cambridge, MA: Harvard University Press.

Bayley, David. (2006). *Changing the guard*. New York: Oxford University Press.

Bayley, David. (2006, October). *Police reform: Who done it?* Paper presented at Berkeley Center for Criminal Justice Forum, Berkeley, CA.

Bayley, David, & Shearing, Clifford. (1996). The future of policing. *The Law and Society Review, 30*, 585–606.

Bennis, Warren. (2003). *On becoming a leader* (rev. ed.). Cambridge, MA: Perseus Publishing.

Bennis, Warren, & Biederman, Patricia Ward. (1997). *Organizing genius*. Cambridge, MA: Perseus Books.

Bennis, Warren, & Townsend, Robert. (1995). *Reinventing leadership: Strategies to empower the organization*. New York: William Morrow and Company.

Berman, Greg, & Feinblatt, John. (2005). *Good courts: The case for problem-solving justice*. New York: New Press.

Bevir, Mark, & Krupicka, Ben. (2006, October). *Police reform: Governance and democracy*. Paper presented at Berkeley Center for Criminal Justice Forum, Berkeley, CA.

Bittner, Egnon. (1967). The police on skid-row: A study of peace keeping. *American Sociological Review, 32*: 699–715.

Bittner, Egon. (1970). *The functions of police in modern society*. Washington, DC: U.S. Government Printing Office.

Bouza, Anthony. (1990). *The police mystique: An insider's look at the cops, crime and the criminal justice system*. New York: Plenum Press.

Bratton, William. (1998). *Turnaround: How America's top cop reversed the crime epidemic*. New York: Random House.

Burns, James MacGregor. (2003). *Transforming leadership*. New York: Atlantic Monthly Press.

Cannon, Lou. (1999). *Official negligence: How Rodney King and the riots changed the LAPD*. Boulder, CO: Westview.

Chandler, Alfred D., Jr. (1977). *The visible hand: The managerial revolution in American business*. Cambridge, MA: Belknap Press.

Christie, Nils. (2004). *A suitable amount of crime*. New York: Routledge.

Collins, James C., & Porras, Jerry I. (1994). *Built to last: Successful habits of visionary companies*. New York: Harper Business.

Collins, Jim. (2001). *Good to great*. New York: HarperCollins.

COPS. (2001). *Racially biased policing: A principled response.* Washington, DC: Police Executive Research Forum.

Couper, David C., & Lobitz, Sabine H. (1991). *Quality policing: The Madison experience.* Washington, DC: Police Executive Research Forum.

Covey, Stephen R. (1989). *The 7 habits of highly effective people.* New York: Free Press.

Covey, Stephen R. (1990). *Principle-centered leadership.* New York: Simon & Schuster.

Dahl, Robert A. (1956). *A preface to democratic theory.* Chicago: University of Chicago Press.

De Tocqueville, Alexis. (1990). *Democracy in America.* New York: Vintage Books.

Delattre, Edwin J. (1996). *Character and cops.* Washington, DC: AEI Press.

Ericson, Richard V., & Haggerty, Kevin D. (1997). *Policing the risk society.* Toronto: University of Toronto Press.

Gardner, John W. (1990). *On leadership.* New York: Free Press.

Geller, William A. (1985). *Police leadership in America: Crisis and opportunity.* Chicago: American Bar Association.

Geller, William A., & Toch, Hans. (1996). *Police violence.* New Haven, CT: Yale University Press.

Goldstein, Herman. (1990). *Problem-oriented policing.* New York: McGraw Hill.

Goleman, Daniel, Boyatzis, Richard, & McKee, Annie. (2002). *Primal leadership: Realizing the power of emotional intelligence.* Boston: Harvard Business School Press.

Graper, Elmer D. (1921). *American police administration: A handbook on police organization and methods of administration of American cities.* New York: Macmillan Company.

Greenstein, Fred I. (2001). *The presidential difference: Leadership style from FDR to George W. Bush.* Princeton, NJ: Princeton University Press.

Haberfeld, Maria R. (2002). *Critical issues in police training.* Upper Saddle River, NJ: Prentice Hall.

Haberfeld, Maria R. (2005). *Police leadership.* Upper Saddle River, NJ: Prentice Hall.

Hackman, J. Richard. (2002). *Leading teams: Setting the stage for great performances.* Boston: Harvard Business School Press.

Harris, David A. (2005). *Good cops.* New York: New Press.

Heifetz, Ronald A. (1994). *Leadership without easy answers.* Cambridge, MA: Belknap Press.

Heifetz, Ronald A., & Linsky, Marty. (2002). *Leadership on the line.* Boston: Harvard Business School Press.

Henry, Vincent E. (2002). *The Compstat paradigm.* Flushing, NY: Looseleaf Law Publications.

Jurkanin, Thomas J. (with Hillard, Terry). (2006). *Chicago police: An inside view—The story of Superintendent Terry Hillard.* Springfield, IL: Charles C. Thomas.

Kelling, George L., (1999, October). *"Broken windows" and police discretion.* Washington, DC: U.S. Department of Justice, Office of Justice Programs.

Kerik, Bernard B. (2001). *The lost son: A life in pursuit of justice.* New York: Regan Books.

Kotter, John P. (1996). *Leading change.* Boston: Harvard Business School Press.

Lardner, James, & Reppetto, Thomas. (2000). *NYPD: A city and its police.* New York: Henry Holt and Company.

Lawler, Edward E., III. (1992). *The ultimate advantage: Creating high involvement organization.* San Francisco: Jossey-Bass.

Lax, David A., & James K. Sebenius. (1986). *The manager as a negotiator: Bargaining for cooperation and competitive gain*. New York: Free Press.

Maple, Jack (with Mitchell, Chris). (2000). *The crime fighter: How you can make your community crime-free*. New York: Broadway Books.

Moody, Steven Maynard, & Musheno, Michael. (2005). *Cops, teachers, counselors: Stories from the front lines of public service*. Ann Arbor: University of Michigan Press.

Moore, Mark H. (1995). *Creating public value: Strategic management in government*. Cambridge, MA: Harvard University Press.

Muir, William Ker, Jr. (1979). *Police: Streetcorner politicians*. Chicago: University of Chicago Press.

Muir, William Ker, Jr. (2003). *An understanding of democracy*. Berkeley, California.

Muir, William Ker, Jr. (2006, October). Police and social democracy. Paper presented at Berkeley Center for Criminal Justice Forum, Berkeley, CA.

Murphy, Patrick V. (1974). *A decade of urban police problems*. Sixteenth Annual Wherrett Lecture on Local Government, University of Pittsburgh, Institute of Public Policy.

Murphy, Patrick V., & Plate, Thomas. (1977). *Commissioner: A view from the top of American law enforcement*. New York: Simon & Schuster.

Newburn, Tim, ed. (2005). *Policing: Key readings*. Portland, OR: Willan Publishing.

Perez, Douglas W. (1994). *Common sense about police review*. Philadelphia: Temple University Press.

Pfeffer, Jeffrey. (1992). *Managing with power: Politics and influence in organizations*. Boston: Harvard Business School Press.

Reiner, Robert. (1991). *Chief constables*. Oxford: Oxford University Press.

Selznick, Philip. (1957). *Leadership in administration: A sociological interpretation*. New York: Harper & Row.

Skolnick, Jerome. (1986). *Justice without trial*. New York: MacMillan.

Skolnick, Jerome, & Bailey, David H. (1986). *The new blue line*. New York: Free Press.

Skolnick, Jerome, & Fyfe, James J. (1993). *Above the law: Police and the excessive use of force*. New York: Free Press.

Slansky, David. (2004). *Democracy and the police*. Unpublished manuscript.

Sparrow, Malcolm K. (2000). *The regulatory craft*. Washington, DC: Brookings Institution Press.

Sparrow, Malcolm K., Moore, Mark H., & Kennedy, David M. (1990). *Beyond 911: A new era for policing*. New York: Basic Books.

Stamper, Norm. (2005). *Breaking rank: A top cop's expose of the dark side of American policing*. New York: Nation Books.

Taylor, Ralph B. (2001). *Breaking away from broken windows*. Boulder, CO: Westview Press.

Toch, Hans, Grant, Douglas, and Galvin, Raymond T. (1975). *Agents of change*. New York: John Wiley and Sons.

Trojanowicz, Robert, & Bucqueroux, Bonnie. (1994). *Community policing: How to get started*. Cincinnati, OH: Anderson Publishing.

Tyler, Tom R., & Huo, Yuen J. (2002). *Trust in the law: Encouraging public cooperation with the police and courts*. New York: Russell Sage Foundation.

Useem, Michael. (2001). *Leading up: How to lead your boss so you both win*. New York: Crown Business.

Weisburd, David, & Braga, Anthony A. (2006). *Police innovation: Contrasting perspectives*. Cambridge, UK: Cambridge University Press.

Wilson, James Q. (1968). *Varieties of police behavior: The management of law and order in eight communities.* Cambridge, MA: Harvard University Press.

Wilson, James Q. (1989). *Bureaucracy.* New York: Basic Books.

Wilson, James Q. (1995). *Political organizations.* Princeton, NJ: Princeton University Press.

Wilson, James Q., & Kelling, George. (1982, March). Fixing broken windows. *The Atlantic Monthly, 249*(3), 29–38.

Wuestewald, Todd, Steinheider, Brigitte, & Bayeri, Petra Saskia. (2006, October). *From the bottom up: Sharing leadership in a police agency* [Abstract]. Paper presented at Berkeley Center for Criminal Justice Forum, Berkeley, CA.

Appendix A: Police Chief Participant List

William Bratton
Los Angeles, California
Boston; New York

Lee Brown
Houston, Texas; Atlanta, Georgia;
New York City, New York

David Couper
Madison, Wisconsin

Ron Davis
East Palo Alto, California

Drew Diamond
Tulsa, Oklahoma
Former deputy director, PERF

Dean Esserman
Providence, Rhode Island

Heather Fong
San Francisco, California

Rick Fuentes
New Jersey State Police

Leonard Hamm
Baltimore, Maryland

Ellen Hanson
Lenexa, Kansas

George Hart
Oakland, California

Gil Kerlikowske
Seattle, Washington; Fort Pierce, FL; Port
St. Lucie, FL; Buffalo, NY

William Kolender
San Diego County, California;
Richmond, CA; San Jose, CA

Bill Lansdowne
San Diego, California

Robert Lunney
Edmonton, Alberta, Canada

Chris Magnus
Richmond, California

Joe McNamara
Kansas City, Missouri; San Jose,
California

George Napper
Atlanta, Georgia

Robert Olson
Minneapolis, Minnesota; Yonkers,
New York

Richard Pennington
Atlanta, Georgia; New Orleans,
Louisiana

Jane Perlov
Raleigh, North Carolina

Darrel Stephens
Charlotte–Mecklenburg, North Carolina;
Police Executive Research Forum
(PERF) director
St. Petersburg, FL; Newport News, VA;
Largo, FL

Charlie Sims
Hattiesburg, Mississippi

Frank Straub
White Plains, New York

Wayne Tucker
Oakland, California

Hubert Williams
Newark, New Jersey; Police Foundation
president

Appendix B:
Demographics of
Police Chiefs' Cities

Police Chief	Location	Region Type	Estimated City Population (2006)	Fiscal Year Police Department Budget	Fiscal Year	Number of Officers	Population per Officer	Police Department Spending per Population	Reported Urban Density (People per sq/mi)	City/Land Area (sq mi)
William Bratton	Los Angeles, California	City	3,849,368	$1,227,258,245	2007	9,520	404	$319	8,205	469.1
Lee Brown	Houston, Texas	City	2,144,491	$575,751,853	2007	5,524	388	$268	3,701	579.4
	Atlanta, Georgia	City	486,411	$137,703,417	2008	1,639	297	$283	3,691	132
	New York City, New York	City	8,214,426	$3,933,800,000	2007	35,548	231	$479	27,083	303.3
David Couper	Madison, Wisconsin	City	223,389	$48,507,296	2006	398	561	$217	3,030	67.3
Ron Davis	East Palo Alto, California	Town	29,506	$8,225,765	2006	40	742	$279	11,586	2.5
Drew Diamond	Tulsa, Oklahoma	City	382,872	$87,162,000	2007	593	646	$228	2,152	182.7
Dean Esserman	Providence, Rhode Island	City	175,255	$43,859,389	2006	494	355	$250	9,473	18.5
Heather Fong	San Francisco, California	City	744,041	$399,400,000	2007	2,092	356	$537	15,834	46.7
Rick Fuentes (State Police)	New Jersey	State	8,724,560	$300,478,000	2007	2,963	2,945	$34	1,134	7428.4
Leonard Hamm	Baltimore, Maryland	City	640,961	$290,993,062	2005	3,906	164	$454	8,058	80.8
Ellen Hanson	Lenexa, Kansas	Town	43,434	$13,429,921	2007	86	505	$309	1,266	34.3
George Hart	Oakland, California	City	415,492	$216,000,000	2007	803	517	$520	7,126	56.1
Gil Kerlikowske	Seattle, Washington	City	582,174	$197,606,055	2007	1,274	457	$339	6,901	83.87
William Kollender (Sheriff)	San Diego County, California	County	2,813,833	$524,000,000	2007	4,000	703	$186	671	4,200
Bill Lansdowne	San Diego, California	City	1,256,951	$360,134,725	2007	2,818	446	$287	3,872	324.3
Robert Lunney	Edmonton, Alberta, Canada	City	836,372	$221,660,000	2007	1,320	634	$265	2,764	264.2

Chief	City	Type	Population	Budget	Year					
Chris Magnus	Richmond, California	Town	103,818	$48,922,134	2006	163	637	$471	3,415	30.4
Joe McNamara	Kansas City, Missouri	City	447,306	$72,442,516	2006	1,359	329	$162	1,407	318
	San Jose, California	City	929,936	$258,288,796	2006	1,789	520	$278	5,216	178.2
George Napper	Atlanta, Georgia	City	486,411	$137,703,417	2008	1,639	297	$283	3,691	132.4
Robert Olson	Minneapolis, Minnesota	City	387,970	$121,248,000	2007	800	485	$313	7,067	54.9
	Yonkers, New York	City	196,086	$69,106,663	2006	687	285	$352	10,834	18.1
Richard Pennington	New Orleans, Louisiana	City	484,674	$99,795,074	2006	1,400	346	$284	2,518	180.6
	Atlanta, Georgia	City	486,411	$137,703,417	2006	1,639	297	$283	3,691	132
Jane Perlov	Raleigh, North Carolina	City	367,995	$67,149,398	2005	851	432	$182	2,409	114.6
Darrel Stephens (PERF director)	Charlotte–Mecklenburg, North Carolina	County	650,000	$127,000,000	2007	1,200	542	$195		
Charlie Sims	Hattiesburg, Mississippi	City	44,779	$11,000,000	2007	140	320	$246	909	49.3
Frank Straub	White Plains, New York	City	53,077	$2,961,826	2007	254	209	$56	5,342	10.4
Wayne Tucker	Oakland, California	City	415,492	$216,000,000	2007	803	517	$520	7,126	56
Hubert Williams	Newark, New Jersey	City	281,402	$133,700,000	2007	1,864	151	$475	11,400	23.8

Appendix C:
Methodology of Study

In my interviews with the police chiefs, I focused on five key leadership areas to analyze how police chiefs provide leadership to their communities and their departments.

First, I asked the chiefs to discuss the importance of police leadership in a democracy. It was important to understand their vision of the department and how it fits into the political, social, and economic structures of the community. I wanted to understand how the chief expresses the department's vision and formulates the role of the department in the delivery of services in the community.

The vision of the police chief was central to this study's analysis of the how the chief developed a strategy to lead the department. In addition, it was important to understand how the chief developed the necessary enforcement and tactical strategies that provide the overall policing approach for the department. This discussion of enforcement strategy was coupled with an in-depth discussion of community-policing approaches, which incorporate both the tactical and community relations strategies central to the contemporary approaches now used in the majority of jurisdictions discussed in this study. Finally, the chiefs discussed their leadership approach to developing departments' culture and norms that support their organizational vision. In many of the interviews, the chiefs discussed the difficult challenge of changing departmental norms and the culture to support a more positive, constructive relationship between the police and the community.

In addition to creating the enforcement and community policing strategies, the chiefs addressed the critical human resources and professional development issues that must be developed in all organization-building efforts. This discussion focused on their recruitment, personnel selection, training, and disciplinary processes, as these are the critical elements that support the fulfillment of any organizational vision. The chiefs discussed specific strategies and organizational programs devised to address the challenges of inappropriate use of force, racial profiling, and integrity and ethics control. These questions were of critical importance in the interviewing process, because a significant share of police literature as well as organizational development materials highlights the importance and difficulty that police organizations have had with the human resources function. This area of professionalism serves as one of the key public indicators of the success or failure of how police leaders manage the balance between enforcement of laws and their demonstrated respect for the public. In addition to these specific human resources issues, the chiefs discussed their own leadership strategies that address police officer motivation and morale. Finally, the chiefs discussed their supervisory dilemmas and their approaches to professional development within the organization.

As the chiefs described their visions and their efforts to develop their internal organization, it was essential to discuss the external and internal political dynamics that impact their departmental vision. Though the external political environment has tremendous impact on the leadership of the police department, it is also clear that in the past 30 years, the advent of police unions has created a new center of political power within the organization. It was critical to understand the impact of this internal power on the successful implementation of the chief's vision for the department. The interviews with the chiefs focused on their ability to mobilize internal political support from line supervisors and senior managers.

The interviews focused on both successes and challenges faced by police leaders. They spoke of their need to balance legal enforcement strategies and their support from the community. The chiefs discussed the difficulties of managing external pressures for reform, such as through federal consent decrees, and public criticism from community leaders. They also discussed the important challenges of the development of police officers, and their views about advanced education and the impact of new technology. Finally, the chiefs discussed personal challenges, and the people and experiences that have shaped their approaches to difficult dilemmas. The interviews allowed the chiefs to discuss their mistakes and take account of the successes in their practice that have enabled them to serve successfully in one or more venues.

The chiefs primarily discussed their experience with their patrol divisions. Though they did not talk about their detective and traffic units specifically, some of the interviews did focus on the importance of these units in support of building better relationships with communities or resolving specific criminal cases.

The overall response to the interviews by the police chiefs was very positive. The stories they shared provide a valuable template for understanding the role of the police chief in a democratic society. This study has been designed to share its findings in a format that will facilitate understanding of the police chief's role amid a variety of issues.

I spent approximately 2 hours with each police leader. The discussions were conducted in a semistructured interview format. In other words, I asked a specific set of questions, but there was also the flexibility for the chiefs to address other issues not directly related to the initial question. The interview was designed to cover each of the five areas of leadership outlined in this section. The majority of the interviews were conducted in the chief's office; only two interviews were completed on the telephone. The chiefs did not have previous access to the interview questions, but discussed each question as presented during the course of the discussion. The chiefs were universally supportive of this study and expressed support for the need to understand and analyze the many challenges that have been and will be faced by police leaders in this country as well as internationally.

Participants

The 26 police chiefs were selected because of their interest in discussing the role of a police chief in our society, my previous knowledge of the chiefs and issues they had confronted, or suggestions from other chiefs about who might offer interesting perspectives. They represented departments of major cities, midsize cities, and a few smaller municipalities. At least nine had served as police executives in more than one department during their police careers.

All of the chiefs were quite receptive to the study and provided at least 1 to 2 uninterrupted hours to complete the interview process. All those invited were willing to participate and answer the questions in a detailed, candid fashion. In addition, per the requirements of the University of California's Office of Human Subject Inquiry regulations, all police chiefs signed the appropriate permission forms that allowed for the public release of their comments for this study.

Data Collection Instrument: Chief Questionnaire

To establish a framework for this study, a police chief leadership question-naire was developed. The questionnaire was reviewed by the chair of my doc-toral committee. In addition, colleagues in the police, social services, and leadership consulting and training fields also reviewed the contents of the questionnaire. The questionnaire was designed to serve as a template for the semistructured interviews. The primary key subject areas that were addressed in the interviews were as follows:

- The chief's vision of policing in a democracy with particular empha-sis on safety concerns and civic decency issues.
- The chief's strategy for developing and implementing the depart-ment's vision.
- The chief's approach to the development of police officers to meet the goals of the department and provide service to the community.

- The chief's methods for coping with external and internal politics of policing in their communities.
- Specific personal reflections on their role as police chief.

Police Chief Leadership Questionnaire Sample

To facilitate the semistructured interview with each of the police chiefs, I developed a set of questions to review with the chiefs. A sample of the questions used in the interviews is given in the following subsections.

Chief's Vision of Police Leadership in a Democracy

What is the role of the police chief in a democracy? Is there a challenge for a police leader to provide a balance between the rights of the citizens and the mandate to provide safety in the community? How have you addressed this challenge in your role as police chief?

How would you define the most important leadership characteristics of a police chief?

What are the key priorities for you during your tenure as police chief?

How do you see the role of the police officer now and into the future?

Describe the challenges that chiefs face in successfully balancing the demands of enforcement and civic decency? What problems have to be addressed when addressing these challenges?

As a police leader, how do you determine the culture of your department? How did you create a police culture and norms to support your vision? How did you do this and what negative norms did you have to address to gather support for your vision?

What was your wish list, that is, the key initiatives that you really wanted to accomplish during your tenure? What were the obstacles that you had to face that impacted your achievement of your goals?

Police Chief's Strategy for Implementing the Vision

What were the key enforcement issues that you faced as police chief?

What has been the impact of the broken windows and zero tolerance strategies of policing on crime reduction, citizens' rights, and community support for the police? How have these approaches impacted your vision of policing?

If you describe yourself as a proponent of community policing, how would you define it and how did you implement this approach in your department? Has this strategy achieved the goals that it was designed to address?

In many communities, there are high levels of violence, drugs, guns, and gangs. How does community policing address these challenges and what impact does an enforcement-only strategy have on the community?

How does community policing impact the leadership role of the police chief and the line officers? What worked for you when implementing this approach and what were the obstacles and challenges?

What has to be done to mobilize political support for the community policing approach? Do some politicians portray this approach as soft or is it universally accepted by both the community and line officers? If not, why not and how did you respond to these perceptions about this police strategy?

What are the challenges of community policing in a post-9/11 environment? How does this strategy work when dealing with new immigrant communities as well as the advent of gangs and increasing violence in communities?

If you used Compstat (or other accountability mechanisms), what has been the impact of this strategy on resource allocation and departmental leadership? Has this strategy been effective for internal management of enforcement and preventive policing approaches, and what have been the challenges in using this approach?

What were the toughest decisions that you had to make as a police chief and how did these decisions impact the mission of your department?

How did you ensure that citizens' rights were protected during your tenure as police chief? Did you face racial profiling issues or other specific demographic changes in your community that necessitated changes in police strategies?

Egon Bittner wrote that "police have a monopoly on the use of coercive power and force." How do you interpret this statement and how does it impact your leadership of police officers? What specific management controls did you implement to ensure that the use of force was well monitored within the department?

How did you build public support for your vision of the department?

Police Chief's Strategy for Development of Police Officers

Many police professionals have urged the profession to change the recruitment standards so that all new officers would have a college degree. Do you think this is an important reform that would improve the quality and professionalism of police officers? What do you consider the key characteristics for recruiting a good police officer?

What are the primary training and development issues for your department? How have you addressed recruitment challenges?

How have you addressed leadership and supervisory training in your department?

How does the chief actually get the officers to do the job right?

Chester Bernard discusses the importance of recognition as an incentive for employees. What do you think motivates your officers to do the job right? How does your leadership impact this effort?

What are the challenges that you addressed as you established a professionally oriented police department? How have you mobilized community support for the professional development of police officers?

How do you maintain a high level of departmental morale?

Describe a situation that has impacted departmental morale and discuss how you handled it? What methods do you use to build morale and support officers in dealing with challenging situations.

How have you handled the issue of police corruption in your department? What are the biggest challenges for police chiefs when addressing this issue?

How do you handle the internal affairs issues of dealing with "high level of complaint" officers? What processes do you use and are these methods effective? Give an example of a situation that involved "too much enforcement" and the approach you used to deal with this situation?

Most organizational leaders discuss the importance of the supervisor. How do you motivate people to lead and supervise your line police officers?

Internal and External Politics' Impact on the Police Chief

When working with the mayor, what is the mayor's role with the police department? How would you describe your working relationship with the mayor? What works well and what are impediments to getting the job done right?

What are the major challenges that you face working with the mayor and other political leaders? What were your successes and failures?

As a police chief, how did the other criminal justice agencies impact your work? What type of support did you receive from them and what were some of the obstacles that you faced in these relationships?

As a police leader, what has been your role in the development of economic, social, and public safety policies in your community? How actively are you involved with the schools, faith, and business communities?

What is your experience with civilian oversight boards and what is the value of these types of external monitoring organizations? What do you believe is the role of the community in the oversight of the police department? What is the impact of these external boards on the internal politics of the department?

What has been your experience working with police unions? What has been your approach to developing a working relationship with the unions and what have been your successes and failures?

Describe a very difficult departmental challenge and outline how you have mobilized both internal and external political support to confront this issue?

Personal Reflections of the Police Chief

Why did you become a police chief? What were your greatest success and your proudest moment as a chief?

What was the worst mistake that you made as a police chief?

Have the changes that you have made as a chief been sustained or replicated in other departments? If so, why has this occurred?

What is your advice to future police leaders about the role of the police chief?

Describe your mentors and the advice that they have offered you about police leadership. Identify any books, courses, or specific people's ideas that have impacted your role as a police leader.

What are the most important changes that you have experienced during your police career? What has not changed in policing that you believe needs to be addressed by police leaders?

Describe your personal history and why you decided to be a police officer and ultimately a police chief.

Data Analysis of Police Chief Questionnaire

All of the interviews were transcribed to facilitate analysis. I reviewed each interview and highlighted specific answers to the aforementioned questions for incorporation into this study. I further examined the interviews to review their relevance to the police leadership literature as well as to develop specific references to situations and experiences that would provide valuable observations about the role of the police chief. The review of the police chiefs' responses to the questionnaire also offered the opportunity to identify key areas of mutual agreement and identify chiefs who have developed unique or challenging approaches to addressing complicated leadership issues. Further, the analysis of the interviews enabled me to identify some of the key leadership strategies chiefs have used to meet the many challenges of this current era. The questionnaire responses indicate that there are many shared leadership approaches as well as wide diversity of political, social, and community contexts that have to be addressed. The data analysis will assist in developing a set of recommendations addressing issues of future police leadership.

Index